THE PROPHETS ON MAIN STREET

The Prophets on Main Street

Revised and Expanded

J. ELLIOTT CORBETT

JOHN KNOX PRESS
ATLANTA

The paraphrase of Amos has been revised from "Amos Today" which appeared in *The Pulpit*, July 1956.

Library of Congress Cataloging in Publication Data

Corbett, Jack Elliott, 1920–
    The Prophets on Main Street.

    Bibliography: p.
    1. Bible. O.T. Prophets—Paraphrases, English.
2. Prophets. I. Title.
BS1505.7.C67   1977   224   77–79597
ISBN 0–8042–0841–7

© John Knox Press 1965, 1978
Atlanta, Georgia
Printed in the United States of America

TO MARJORIE RUTH CORBETT

PREFACE TO THE SECOND EDITION

In this enlarged edition, two additional prophets were selected for inclusion, Micah and Hosea. In terms of the quality of their oracular utterances, these two eighth century seers measured up to the standards reached by other Hebrew prophets. They feared the doom of Israel and Judah, preached social righteousness, and yet understood that Yahweh was a God of infinite forbearance and steadfast love.

Paraphrases of the teachings of Hosea and Micah have spawned commentaries on such questions as nuclear energy, housing, corruption of the powerful, wiretapping, crime, violence, Vietnam in retrospect and America in prospect.

In addition, new paraphrases have been developed from passages in Isaiah and Jeremiah. Some of these deal with science and religion, hypocrisy, ocean resources, Watergate, hunger, women's rights, citizenship, China, and international development.

An Appendix has been added which includes an Affirmation of Social Faith and an Affirmation of Social Action.

In the Table of Contents an asterisk has been placed before each paraphrase that is new to this edition and did not appear in *The Prophets on Main Street.*

Several of the paraphrases appeared previously in *The Now Prophets,* a study book used by United Methodist Women.

My special thanks goes to my wife, Sarah Anne, and my co-worker, Elizabeth Smith, both of whom typed portions of the manuscript. If a few of the paraphrases appear to be inspired, I am grateful. If some seem quite pedestrian, I am sure God will use other instruments to make his message forceful on these significant subjects. In any event, it is an awesome assignment to attempt to be a spokesperson for God to one's own times. The prophets of the eighth, seventh and sixth centuries B.C. performed this role exceedingly well. I invite you—in the spirit of Amos, Hosea, and Micah—to put your hand to writing the word the world needs to hear.

Jack Corbett
February 1977

INTRODUCTION TO THE FIRST EDITION

The Old Testament prophets were not crystal-ball gazers. When they prophesied under the inspiration of God, they spoke most frequently about the appalling social conditions of their day. They were not foretellers; they were forth-tellers. It was not their mission to forecast events but to speak on behalf of God in the context of their times. This does not mean that the prophets were unconcerned about the future. They predicted prosperity or devastation, peace or war, depending upon the degree of moral responsibility of king and people before God.

Lonely men, the prophets were often religious leaders without followers, although sometimes they had a few disciples. In the countryside, on the hilltop, or out in the desert, they especially felt the presence of God. But it was when witnessing to the flagrant violation of God's will in the cities that they could not contain themselves. Like Jeremiah, they were "weary with holding it in." (Jer. 20:9) Or, like Second Isaiah, they attested, "He made my mouth like a sharp sword." (Isa. 49:2)

It is difficult for us to understand the anguish in the hearts of the prophets. Because they were very close to the people, when it was necessary for them to pronounce judgment they took no sadistic pleasure in it. Rather, they must have winced under the lash of their own tongues and cringed under the hammer blows of their own words. Often they begged God to stay his anger.

Their purpose as instruments of God was to redeem rather than to proclaim judgment. They wanted their people to turn from sin rather than reap the consequences of their disobedience. They brooded over the people and wept over resistant spirits, much as Jesus wept over Jerusalem for its rejection of his teachings.

The prophets were often despised, sometimes feared, but always respected. What they had said proved upon the reflection of later generations to be true. In bane and blessing their prophecies were fulfilled.

What has been attempted in the paraphrases of this volume is not to rewrite the Scriptures, but to make the prophetic material more meaningful to our contemporary society. The accomplishment of a similar objective is the aim of every sermon. It is hoped that readers of this book will be moved to return to the prophets and ponder their deeper meanings for our own times.

I have made no attempt to "Phillippize" the Old Testament. Only J. B. Phillips in his inimitable way can summon the appropriate language for this task. In the process of paraphrasing seven prophetic books, the question uppermost in my mind has been, "What would the prophets, given their spirit, be inclined to say about this matter today?" The theological position of the prophets has been generally preserved, but I have attributed to them some further spiritual insights as a result of the twenty-five centuries of human experience that have intervened. For this reason the theology may be less judgmental and will depend more upon the impartial operation of divine law than upon direct intervention by an aroused deity.

Six of the paraphrases are in free verse while Jonah is written in satirical narrative. In other words, the paraphrases are framed in the form in which they were originally cast. All of the paraphrases deal with current religious, social, and political problems, with an emphasis upon international affairs. I have attempted to preserve the spirit and passion of the prophets as they would view today's scene, but I have avoided sticking slavishly to the original text.

For the observant reader there will be obvious omissions. These are not studied omissions; they exist only because the passages did not strike fire at the time of writing. Subject matter has also been included which has no close counterpart in the original prophets, including such subjects as Communism, race, and the Peace Corps. These, however, represent the kind of significant topics the ever alert prophets would be apt to consider today.

It was not originally planned to include a treatment of the "suffering servant" theme. To deal with this poem would be tantamount to an ancient Hebrew touching the Ark of the Covenant, so it seemed. However, as the tempo of the non-violent direct action movement for racial freedom quickened, the theme appeared too timely to omit.

Admittedly the transition points between paraphrases are not always smooth. Perhaps it is in this respect that I have been most true to the prophets! Also in the writings of the Old Testament it is not always clear when a prophet speaks in his own name and when he is speaking an oracle of the Lord. I do not presume in these paraphrases to claim that anything that is written is on the "oracle" level. I can only hope that it is not contrary to the will of God.

I would like to emphasize that the contemporary paraphrases as framed in this volume are not conceived to be the last word—or even the next to the last word. Rather, it is hoped that each reader will be encouraged to go back to the Bible and try his own hand at the adaptation of the message of the prophets to the rapidly changing modern scene.

Where Scripture material is used directly in the paraphrased sections, it appears in the text in italics. Biblical references for the paraphrases are indicated with the titles and in parentheses, should the reader wish to consult the source in its original context. The Revised Standard Version of the Bible has been used throughout.

Some readers already thoroughly familiar with the life and times of the prophets may wish to turn directly to the paraphrases themselves. Most readers will find it advantageous to read the brief commentaries for each book of prophecy and to familiarize themselves with the selections of scriptural material preceding the paraphrases.

I wish to record a note of appreciation to those who have read the paraphrases and who have made helpful suggestions: Dr. Lowell B. Hazzard, The Reverend J. Emery Fleming, and my colleague, The Reverend W. Rodney Shaw. They, of course, are not responsible for the shortcomings that I am sure exist in this volume.

I feel greatly indebted to my Old Testament professor, Dr. James B. Pritchard, who first stirred my excitement over the prophets. Last, but most important of all, thanks to my wife who originally suggested that I attempt to place the prophets on Main Street.

CONTENTS

*This indicates new material in this edition.
Each chapter will be preceded by a full contents.

I | AMOS

*This indicates new material in this edition

Amos—His Time and Ours

THE LIFE AND TIMES OF AMOS

Amos was a layman. Unlike many of the other prophetic figures, he had no formal education. He had received no special training in either his religious heritage or literary technique. Although a citizen of the Southern Kingdom of Judah, he proclaimed his message in the streets of the Northern Kingdom of Israel. Though branded as an "outside agitator" by the religious leaders of Israel, the people listened to his message and he succeeded in "getting under their skin."

The home of Amos was in the wilderness of Tekoa, a bleak area of limestone hills about six miles south of Jerusalem. Meager vegetation provided scant pasturage for Amos' small flock of sheep. He barely mustered a living by laboring also as a dresser of sycamore (fig) trees, the pricking of whose fruit encouraged ripening. Seeking a market for his products in the larger trading centers of Israel, Amos traveled to the cities of Bethel, Gilgal, Samaria, and even Damascus.

The luxurious living he observed in these cities appalled and deeply troubled him. The lack of concern by the well-to-do for the oppressed and unfortunate aroused his anger. Amos was moved to speak out bluntly and forthrightly in the name of God against injustice.

The lowly shepherd of Tekoa may have seemed ill-equipped to issue divine pronouncements in cities where prophets were trained in fluency of speech and where many of his hearers were far better educated than he. But Amos had an educated heart, and under the compelling power of the Spirit of God he spoke some of the most striking, terse, direct, and passionately poetic lines to be found in all the Bible.

THE KINGDOM OF ISRAEL UNDER JEROBOAM II

The ministry of Amos occurred during the long reign of Jeroboam II (786–746 B.C.). It was a time of great prosperity and substantial security for the Northern Kingdom of Israel. During the early years of Jeroboam's reign, Assyria had defeated Syria, but was in such need of recovery from that blood-letting struggle that Israel was left relatively free. Under Jeroboam II, Israel reached the height of its territorial expansion. Trade flowed along the routes running through many cities of Israel. The upper classes owned both winter houses and summer houses and decorated them with ivory. The people felt that such good times were strong evidence of Yahweh's favor. They reciprocated in turn by offering their choicest animals for sacrifice and by participating in religious celebrations with at least outward loyalty.

Yet all was not well in Israel. Under the influence of the Canaanite fertility cults, sacred prostitution had become commonplace. Religious festivals degenerated into occasions for gluttony and drunkenness. Merchants, in order to make a high profit, sold wheat mixed with chaff. The poor, so completely at the mercy of the wealthy classes, were often sold into slavery to pay for their debts.

What disturbed Amos most was the silence of the prophets. Instead of raising their voices in protest they often descended to the level of debauchery themselves. "You made the Nazirites drink wine," cried Amos, "and commanded the prophets, saying, 'You shall not prophesy.' " (2:12) Amos could contain himself no longer.

THE MAJOR TEACHINGS OF AMOS

One of the major truths Amos sought to communicate to the people of Samaria was that *God rules over and judges all nations.* As the prophet denounces the transgressions of their neighbors—Damascus, Gaza, Tyre, Edom, Ammon, Moab, and even Judah—one can almost visualize the Israelites smiling smugly and nodding their heads. If Amos had only stopped there, he could have retained his popularity as the ancient counterpart of a modern Soviet demonologist. But instead he went on to devastatingly describe the moral failure of the Israelites themselves, which equally deserved terrifying judgment.

It was not as though the Israelites had not had abundant opportunity to repent. Frequently they had been chastened by the Lord—through famine, drought, blight, and pestilence, yet despite all this, said the spokesman for God, "you did not return to me." (4:6–11) Because you went your own way, ignoring all warnings, there is nothing left for you now except to "prepare to meet your God." (4:12)

Amos saw the people under a double judgment. They not only knew better, but they were living under the covenant which God had made with them when he delivered them from Egypt. They were therefore expected to be more responsible and disciplined, yet they had betrayed the Almighty. Many Israelites felt that when the day of the Lord came, it would be a day of triumph and rejoicing, a day when God would bestow his special benefits upon them. But Amos corrected this misconception. Because of their behavior, the day of the Lord would be for them a day of darkest gloom with no brightness in it.

Still another principle which Amos preached to Israel was that *Yahweh demanded righteousness above religiosity.* When the people came on three-day pilgrimages to Bethel and Gilgal, purportedly to bring their sacrifices, tithes, and freewill offerings, they spent much of their time in gross wickedness (4:4, 5). Ritual replaced righteousness and became a mere cover-up for transgression. Pilgrimages to the shrines of the unholy cities were blatant hypocrisy.

Amos proclaimed that the Lord despised their "solemn assemblies" and their religious feasts which had become occasions for gluttony. Burnt offerings, cereal offerings, and peace offerings are no substitute for a penitent heart. What God truly desires is that "justice roll down like waters, and righteousness like an everlasting stream."

A primary strain running throughout the book of Amos is that *the Lord condemns social sin.* Personal corruption had become so embedded in the customs of society that many licentious practices were accepted by the community without a second thought. "It must be all right," the people said, "everybody does it." Amos was unmistakably blunt in speaking about the injustices of society which he felt broke the heart of God. He was especially displeased with the wealthy landowner class who "trampled upon the poor." Apparently they kept their farm laborers in a quasi-indentured servant status, requiring such a large share of the wheat harvest that the workers were always in debt. Amos objected to the rich building both summer and winter houses for themselves when so many of the poor had not so much as a shelter for over their heads.

Amos pronounced his woes against the ostentatious leisure class who amused themselves in bored sophistication, but were not "grieved over the ruin of Joseph." These irresponsible "opulent beatniks" neither knew nor cared that Israel was on the brink of destruction. The idle rich women, unconcerned over the lot of the poor, were scorned by Amos as "cows of Bashan." He minced no words in warning the eighth-century counterpart of the female cocktail set of the disaster impending for the corrupt capital city of Samaria. Like the carcasses of dead animals, he predicted, their corpses would be removed from the ruined city (Samaria was sacked by the Assyrians not many years later, 722–721 B.C.).

Nor did the politicians escape the observing eye of Amos. They were willing to "take a bribe" even if it meant forsaking the interests of their decent constituents. The merchants were also condemned who in their greed could not wait for the Sabbath to pass so they could get back to their unscrupulous business practices. Like the dishonest butcher who puts his hand on the scale, the wheat merchants dealt "deceitfully with false balances." They made the measure small and the price great. Fraudulent profits were in turn used to compound evil—to buy the poverty-stricken as slaves for a few silver coins, and "the needy for a pair of sandals."

Against the backdrop of these injustices, Amos reveals his vision of the Lord with a plumb line in his hand. He is setting the plumb line in the midst of the house of Jacob, a house with sagging walls, about to collapse.

In chapter nine Amos describes the attempts of the desperate Israelites to escape destruction. He warns those who comfort themselves that they will get away safely if disaster should come. Whether they dig into Sheol, climb up to heaven, hide on a mountain or at the bottom of the sea, the Lord who commands the heavens and the earth will find them and bring them under judgment.

We need to remember that in spite of Amos' dire predictions of doom, his purpose was not to terrify the people or to glory in their punishment. He preached that they might repent. "Seek the Lord and live." Had the people turned from their sins, no one in Israel would have offered more joyous prayers of thanksgiving than Amos.

What was the reaction of Israel to the bold pronouncements of the shepherd of Tekoa? The priest of Bethel, Amaziah, reported Amos to King Jeroboam as guilty of conspiracy. The complaint of the priest was not that Amos uttered untruth, but that "the land is not able to bear all his words." (7:10) He suggested that Amos go home to Judah where he belonged. "Prophesy there; but never again prophesy at Bethel." (7: 12–13) In other words, your prophecies are an embarrassment to the elite here, for "it is the king's sanctuary." (7:13)

We do not know what happened to Amos, whether he was stoned to death or whether he went back to his home in Judah. But whatever happened, his appraisal of eighth-century Israel was so correct and his judgment so far-sighted that later generations preserved his prophetic witness. His words stand today to judge another generation.

AMOS' MESSAGE FOR THE MODERN ERA

Several general principles proclaimed by Amos are particularly pertinent to our own nation today. One of these, restated, is: *The United States must expect to be judged by God and his moral law on the basis of its own behavior.* Although we have been blessed by God as a nation, no more than Israel can we expect to receive preferred status. For God, as Amos declared, is the Judge of *all* nations. Too often we have adopted the double standard of judging the Soviets either by their unseemly actions or by the damning words of some long-dead Communist prophet, and judging ourselves by our good intentions and the idealism of the Declaration of Independence.

Some examples of how reluctant we are to judge our own nation objectively, as God must judge us, include the following:

1. It was only when Soviet missile bases were discovered on Cuban soil that many Americans for the first time were able to grasp the fear felt by

the Russian people because of our advance missile bases in places like Turkey, directly on the border of the Soviet Union. Now, of course, our Jupiter missiles, old-fashioned and good only for first-strike, have been removed from Turkey and Italy.

2. Generally speaking, we claim to believe in free trade. Nevertheless, when Italian shoes become popular imports or Japanese-produced color TV sets compete successfully with those produced in the U.S., then we cry for tariff protection. Yet if a foreign government placed a tariff against American-built computers sold overseas, to safeguard their own industry, we would probably complain about discriminatory practices.

3. In 1946 the U.S. Senate adopted the Connally Amendment. This reservation was attached to our acceptance of the compulsory jurisdiction of the International Court of Justice. This "self-judging clause" means that we reserve the right to determine in advance whether or not a case in which we are involved ought to be submitted to the World Court. It thus appears to other nations that we wish to remain a law unto ourselves rather than being willing to risk a possible adverse decision by submitting all justiciable cases to this international body.

4. When American arms help to implement military coups in such places as the Dominican Republic and Honduras, surely then our use of military assistance to "strengthen the free world" needs to be brought into question.

We ought to be cognizant of another contemporary application of Amos' teaching: *The church cannot allow ritual, financial affairs, building programs, or other secondary matters to interfere with the implementation of righteousness.* Elaborate forms of worship, mass rallies, suppers, new organs, or large collections sometimes seem to be the most important matters in the life of a church. Then we read Amos again and discover that God desires justice and righteousness more than feasts, solemn assemblies, ritual, offerings, and fine music (5:21–24).

We may believe that if we remodel the sanctuary, install a communion rail, secure new altar cloths, and bedeck the minister in colorful vestments, something significant has been achieved for the kingdom. Actually in such a priestly environment the preacher may feel it inappropriate to utter the prophetic messages the people most need to hear.

When we deplore the plight of the Russian Orthodox Church today under the restrictions imposed by a Communist government, we should recall that this same church before the 1917 revolution found its major expression in liturgical worship and elaborate ritual. The church then showed little compassion for the serfs, nor did it speak out against cruel practices of government officials or the luxury-loving aristocracy. Instead most of the priests were concerned with gold-leafing their church domes and so bejewelling their lectern Bibles that it required extreme effort to open the Book to read such prophets as Amos!

Christians who would heed Amos' message must always be seeking ways to establish justice in their communities, in the courts, in business, in political and social life. They will strive to improve race relations, to meet welfare needs adequately, to promote mental health, to provide good schools and recreational outlets. As St. Paul admonished the Christians in Rome: "Offer your bodies in a *living* sacrifice . . . that is your rational worship." (Rom. 12:1, Goodspeed, italics mine)

Amos' message might be applied in still another way to contemporary times: *Christians must be concerned about sin in society as well as about personal morality.* To be a bank embezzler or a murderer is to be considered sinful by the majority of people. But if a shrewd entrepreneur organizes a combine of corporations in such a way as to enrich the board of directors without paying dividends to the stockholders, he or she may be thought of as a financial wizard. Or in wartime, if a plane bombs the enemy nation, killing thousands of innocent citizens, both the pilot and the bombardier may be rewarded for heroism. As Dr. Reinhold Niebuhr said years ago: "There is an increasing tendency among modern men to imagine themselves ethical because they have delegated their vices to larger and larger groups."[1]

Alcoholism is a personal problem for some nine million individuals in our nation, yet it is closely related to such social problems as crime, delinquency, poverty, and automobile accidents. For example, research by the National Safety Council indicates that "drinking is indicated to be a factor in at least half of the fatal motor-vehicle accidents . . ."[2] From 1963 to 1973, the period during the Vietnam War, there were 577,848 Americans killed in auto deaths. Fifty percent of this number (those related to alcohol) would be 288,924. Yet, by comparison, during the same years 46,121 U.S. soldiers were killed in Vietnam.[3] Thus, one can easily see that in eleven years on the highway there were five times as many alcohol-related deaths as there were fatalities in the entire Vietnam conflict over the same period. Yet we Americans do not become righteously indignant, but continue to tolerate a profusion of roadside drinking places, primarily accessible by automobile.

Residential segregation is perhaps the greatest social sin in the United States today. A study of church members in a white suburban area of Los Angeles indicated that more than one-half of the Christians polled would disapprove of a black family of similar education and income moving into their neighborhood. Integrating of schools and of church congregations can be expected to be no more than token so long as residential segregation is a continuing policy. As Dr. Roger Ragan states: "Perhaps local churches have talked too much about getting their own houses in order to the neglect of community conditions which make it next to impossible for them to be inclusive."[4]

If Amos were living today he would surely be concerned about the predicament of the chronically poor: the illiterate, unskilled outcasts of our affluent nation. He would be indignant at the comfortable middle-class citizens and the tax-conscious politicians who rejoice in slashing the relief rolls. He might urge them instead to invest enough resources in rehabilitation so that such families could become self-respecting contributors to society, instead of perpetuating poverty from generation to generation.

Undoubtedly the shepherd from Tekoa would challenge many of our accepted social practices. He might probe into situations that others considered none of his business. Yet the prophet Amos would not easily be silenced by those who denounced him as a "meddling outside agitator."

Selections from Amos

Thus says the LORD:
"For three transgressions of Gaza,
   and for four, I will not revoke the punishment;
because they carried into exile a whole people
   to deliver them up to Edom.
So I will send a fire upon the wall of Gaza,
   and it shall devour her strongholds. . . ."
Thus says the LORD:
"For three transgressions of Edom,
   and for four, I will not revoke the punishment;
because he pursued his brother with the sword,
   and cast off all pity . . ."
Thus says the LORD:
"For three transgressions of Judah,
   and for four, I will not revoke the punishment;
because they have rejected the law of the LORD,
   and have not kept his statutes,
but their lies have led them astray,
   after which their fathers walked.
So I will send a fire upon Judah,
   and it shall devour the strongholds of Jerusalem."

Thus says the LORD:
"For three transgressions of Israel,
   and for four, I will not revoke the punishment;
because they sell the righteous for silver,
   and the needy for a pair of shoes—
they that trample the head of the poor into the dust of the earth,
   and turn aside the way of the afflicted . . ."

"Hear this word, you cows of Bashan,
   who are in the mountain of Samaria,
who oppress the poor, who crush the needy,

who say to their husbands, 'Bring, that we may drink!'
The Lord GOD has sworn by his holiness
    that, behold, the days are coming upon you,
when they shall take you away with hooks,
    even the last of you with fishhooks.
And you shall go out through the breaches,
    every one straight before her;
and you shall be cast forth into Harmon,"* says the LORD.

WHAT GOD DESIRES 5:21–24

I hate, I despise your feasts,
    and I take no delight in your solemn assemblies.
Even though you offer me your burnt offerings and cereal offerings,
    I will not accept them,
and the peace offerings of your fatted beasts
    I will not look upon.
Take away from me the noise of your songs;
    to the melody of your harps I will not listen.
But let justice roll down like waters,
    and righteousness like an ever-flowing stream.

THE PROPHET'S CALL 7:14–15

Then Amos answered Amaziah, "I am no prophet, nor a prophet's son; but I am a herdsman, and a dresser of sycamore trees, and the LORD took me from following the flock, and the LORD said to me, 'Go, prophesy to my people Israel.' "

THE GREEDY MERCHANTS 8:4–6

Hear this, you who trample upon the needy,
    and bring the poor of the land to an end,
saying, "When will the new moon be over,
    that we may sell grain?
And the sabbath,
    that we may offer wheat for sale,
that we may make the ephah small and the shekel great,
    and deal deceitfully with false balances,
that we may buy the poor for silver
    and the needy for a pair of sandals,
    and sell the refuse of the wheat?"

*The refuse pile.

THE RESTORATION OF ISRAEL 9:13–15

"Behold, the days are coming," says the LORD,
"When the plowman shall overtake the reaper
and the treader of grapes him who sows the seed;
the mountains shall drip sweet wine,
and all the hills shall flow with it.
I will restore the fortunes of my people Israel,
and they shall rebuild the ruined cities and inhabit them;
they shall plant vineyards and drink their wine,
and they shall make gardens and eat their fruit.
I will plant them upon their land,
and they shall never again be plucked up
out of the land which I have given them,"

says the LORD your God.

Amos—Prophet of Justice in an Atomic Age

Thus says the Lord:
For three transgressions of Germany, and for four,
    I will not turn it back;
for you have destroyed millions in your gas chambers,
    and persecuted my people without pity.
Therefore a wall shall divide you,
    and foreign nations shall occupy you.
For three transgressions of Japan, and for four,
    I will not turn it back,
because you ravaged your neighbors,
    and oppressed the weak through conquest.
So I will make of you an armed camp and a naval base,
    though in your constitution you outlaw war.
For three transgressions of Russia, and for four,
    I will not turn it back,
for you have kept your people in ignorance by censorship,
    and falsely convinced them of their prosperity.
You have rattled your missiles above the noisy proclamations of your
        peaceful intentions,
    and tampered with the freedom of friendly nations.
So I will tip your hand to your opponents,
    and saddle your people with the heavy burden of armaments.
For three transgressions of America, and for four,
    I will not turn it back,
because you have dropped atom bombs without remorse upon open
        cities,
    and stockpiled H-bombs ad infinitum.
So I will make other nations fear your power and envy your wealth.
Your doom is assured, your demise is at hand.
For I hear your songs of self-praise;
    I listen also to your criticism of others.
But though I remove the wax from my straining ears,
    I cannot hear your voice raised in self-judgment or repentance.
There is wailing in the streets of Washington,
    and confusion on the expressways of Chicago.

There is atomic dust over the city of Los Angeles;
   no smog lay as heavy or as long.
The cries of children in New York City
   are heard above the siren's scream.
For you trusted in the makers of atom bombs,
   but not in the Maker of the atom.

IDLE IRRESPONSIBILITY (6:4–7)

Hear this word, you who while away the idle hours, saying,
   "When will the next bingo game be played?" or
   "What club shall we go to tonight?"
Woe unto you who go to deep freezers, saying,
   "Shall it be steak or chicken?"
   but care little for my children in India who have no rice.
For I will take away what you think you have,
   and give it to those who have none.

THE VENEER OF PIETY (5:21–24)

I hate your new church buildings,
   I take no great pleasure in your rising membership rolls.
The tinkle of your treasuries gives me an earache!
   Take away from my sight your veneer of piety.
To your boasts of being a Christian nation I will not listen.
But let justice roll down like waters,
   and righteousness like an ever-flowing stream.

A REFUGE FOR THE FEW

Woe unto you unless you search after *my* ways
   and follow after *my* commandments!
Your grandfathers found America a haven for the many,
   but you have made it a refuge for the few.
Your poetry at the gate says,
   "Give me your tired, your poor,
   your huddled masses yearning to be free."
But your law at the gate says,
   "Your nationality is wrong,
   your language is wrong,
   your color is wrong,
   you were born in the wrong place—
   stay home, Puerto Ricans!"

ALCOHOL + GASOLINE = BLOOD

Woe unto you, hypocrites! who tolerate TV beer commercials
   to·sponsor your national sport,
yet you are puzzled when teen-agers turn for enjoyment
   from baseball to beer-drinking.
You clutter your highways with taverns,
   though when alcohol and gasoline are mixed,
   too often they turn to blood.
You piously proclaim, "What's the harm in a little drink?"
Yet you show only disgust at the skid-row plight
   of millions of dead-end alcoholics.

AN ORACLE CONCERNING INTERNATIONAL DEVELOPMENT (9:13)

Hear this word, O Americans!
During this century more humans died of starvation
   than were killed by the ravages of war.
What will you do in thirty years
   when the inhabitants of the earth are doubled?
I had a terrifying vision of grey shadows in three dimensions:
   each year around the globe
   millions of children reaching the age
   when due to malnutrition their mentality becomes permanently
      impaired.

On them food supplements are lost.
   No steak, nor cheese, nor spinach
   can restore what is gone forever.
O yogurt-eating Americans!
Can your stomachs imagine undernourishment?
Do you condemn the poor as simply lazy?
Could *you* work for a week on one day's food?

Can you face this fact:
   that developing nations could now absorb four billion dollars
      more in aid—
And simultaneously slash your gifts to international assistance,
   while your Gross National Product soars?
Is your compassion in inverse ratio to your wealth?

If trade benefits needy nations ten times as much as aid,
   why do you restrict it?
You beat a man with one hand while you dress his wounds with the other!

O Developing Nations!
   Is family planning an imperialist plot to control you?
   Or an avenue to your economic independence?
   You are wise enough to establish death controls,
      but not flexible enough to accept birth controls.

What are you doing to help yourselves?
Are you eager to receive aid from abroad
   but reluctant to levy taxes at home?
Are you quick to accept grants of grain,
   but slow to enforce land reform?
Do you request World Bank loans
   yet not restrict the flight of capital overseas?
Do you ask for power plants and airports
   before fertilizer and water pumps?

O Brazil!
Your one-crop economy is enough to give us all
   coffee nerves!

O Colombia!
Why do you graze thousands of cattle in the fertile valleys,
   while your peasants till the rocky hillsides?

O Egypt!
Why do you squander human resources on hate,
   and material resources on war?

Woe unto you, India!
Where rats devour more than all your food imports,*
and in the name of religion, cattle eat while humans starve.

O America, my beloved!
Catalyst for the Marshall Plan,
launcher of the Peace Corps,
initiator of the Alliance for Progress,
supporter of world missions,
   are your good works all in the past tense?

Why are you so generous with your military aid?
   So Latin American armies can intimidate elected presidents?
   So India and Pakistan can battle over Kashmir?

*Most losses consist of domestically raised grain and occur in the field. The Indian Bambikoot rat is a very hardy creature thriving in irrigation canal banks, and thus far no effective bait system has been developed.

So a Greek army can overturn democracy?

Makers of foreign policy!
Would you put a dime in a beggar's cup if anyone saw you?
Can you admit to benevolent motives, in response to humanity's need?
   Or must all charitable impulses be subordinate to realism:
      "It's good for U.S. business."
      "It will develop future customers."
      "It will help combat communism."

One hundred per cent Americans!
   Would you shorten my hand?
   Tailor compassion to politics?
     "How do they vote in the UN?"
     "Are their leaders friendly?"
     "Do they trade with our enemies?"

Are these nations' children to be sentenced to hunger,
   their farmers strapped to wooden plows,
   their mothers burdened with endless childbearing?

O Members of Congress!
Your tongues are calloused from debating foreign aid.
   Who will be the toughest with nations struggling to be neutral?
   Who will win the prize for restrictive amendments?
   Who will be victor in punishing the unappreciative?

*   *   *   *   *

"Behold, the days are coming," says the Lord,
   "when the plowman shall overtake the reaper,
   and the treader of grapes him who sows the seed;
the mountains shall drip sweet wine,
   and all the hills shall flow with it."
Let that day march forth!
   when the commands of Christ are obeyed:
     the hungry are taught to grow crops
     the thirsty are drilling wells
     the sick are being cured
     those imprisoned by illiteracy are set free!
Let that day break!
   when people freed from gnawing hunger can think again,
   when those cured of malaria have strength to till the land,
   when every man may sit under his own fig tree,
     and under the roof of a house he owns.

PRIVILEGE-SEEKERS

Your farmers want cushioning price supports,
    your corporate heads seek cost-plus contracts;
your unions guaranteed annual wages,
    your veterans lobby for special privileges.
Yet a cry goes up from the same people:
    "Down with high prices! Down with inflation! Down with big
       government!"
Every pressure group among you wants cake—
    but let the other person pay for it.

THE RACE IN SPACE

Hear this word,
you who shoot rockets out into space!
    Have you solved all problems on your earth?
Is it prestige you seek to buttress your unsure confidence?
    Do you expect to impress the third of the world that is
       uncommitted,
      those less-developed nations who are hungry, illiterate, and
       diseased?
Bend your ear, O America! Do not be deceived!
The space *they* care about
    is their empty stomachs;
the shots that will most impress *them*
    are penicillin shots!

CALL OF THE PROPHET (7:14–15)

I am not a called preacher who must depend for my security
    upon those who hire me;
who must please the people of the pews,
    but not necessarily the God of the heavens.
My calling is of God, for I am only a poor shepherd
    and the pruner of fruit trees.
But *the Lord took me from following the flock, and the Lord
said to me, "Go, prophesy to my people* of America."

II | *HOSEA

HIS TIMES AND OURS

SELECTIONS FROM HOSEA

PROPHET OF FORGIVING LOVE

*All material in this part is new in this edition

Hosea—His Times and Ours

HISTORICAL SETTING

Hosea prophesied in the Northern Kingdom of Israel after the time of Amos. He sometimes refers to Israel as "Ephraim" which was a major province and included cities of Samaria and Shechem.

His work began before the death of Jeroboam II (746 B.C.) and before the raid of Assyrian king Tiglath-Pileser III on Gilead and Galilee (733 B.C.). He preached between about 760 and 735 B.C. At that time Israel was in a state of anarchy. In the ten years immediately following Jeroboam's death, she had five kings, three of whom had seized the throne by violence. Death was everywhere. Hosea's repugnant reaction to all this bloody violence was to say: "A vulture is over the house of the Lord!"

Hosea knew his country and its geography. He was also a keen observer of nature and of life going on around him. As Mary Ellen Chase writes: "He observed the skies, their clouds, the doves and the eagles, the foam upon the swollen streams after the rains, the dew upon the fields, just as he watched the bakers at their ovens, the craftsmen melting heathen images into shape, the builders working upon their temples to foreign gods."[1] He made references in his oracles to all of these sights and sounds.

HOSEA'S MARRIAGE

Hosea was told by the Lord to marry a girl named Gomer, whom he loved. In the second verse of Hosea, Gomer is referred to as a "wife of harlotry." But Abraham Heschel points out in *The Prophets* that the Hebrew meaning does not connote a harlot—but rather a person *disposed* to be a harlot.

For a while their marriage was a happy one. They had three children, each called by a symbolic name. The first was called Jezreel (where a king of Israel had been killed). The second child was named "Not pitied," and indicated that divine punishment was about to fall on the people of Israel. The third was called "Not my people" which was meant to declare that the covenant had been broken between the Lord and his people.

Later Hosea discovered that Gomer had been unfaithful to him and had given herself to many lovers. She became a harlot and according to the law, Hosea could not live with her. Eventually she was sold into slavery.

As Heschel points out, God's way is higher than the legal way. Thus, the Lord said to Hosea about Gomer: "Go again, love a woman who is beloved of a paramour and is an adulteress; even as the LORD loves the people of Israel though they turn to other gods." (3:1) So Hosea bought Gomer out of slavery and took her back to his house as his wife. He did not forsake her despite her unfaithfulness and the anguish she had caused him.

Hosea compared his personal experience with God's attitude toward unfaithful Israel, and declared that God was ready to express forgiving love if his people would but return to him.

TEACHINGS OF HOSEA

Like Amos who prophesied in the same area a few years before him, Hosea spoke out dramatically concerning the sins of the people of Israel. This is perhaps most clearly seen in the opening verses of the fourth chapter of the book. Hosea proclaims that "the Lord has a controversy with the inhabitants of the land."

He declares:

> There is no faithfulness or kindness,
>   and no knowledge of God in the land;
> there is swearing, lying, killing, stealing and committing adultery;
>   they break all bounds and murder follows murder. (4:1, 2)

The Lord is angry because there is no fidelity or steadfastness. Nor is there basic kindness, which here means "covenant love," or a feeling of fellowship with God between two who have, in the spirit of trust, accepted certain obligations. Not only that but there is a basic ignorance of God's law. Hosea mentions "swearing" by which he must mean false swearing —the taking of an oath without any serious intention of carrying it out. He then specifies four other sins which conform to those particularized in the sixth, seventh, eighth, and ninth of the Ten Commandments. John Mauchline comments that "by Hosea's time the Decalogue may have been formulated and recognized as a standard of conduct."[2]

Hosea emphasizes something else in his teaching: God is concerned over Israel's idolatry. What the people are doing now borders on the occult. They "inquire of a thing of wood, and their staff gives them oracles." (4:12) They consult dead wood instead of the living Lord. He sums it up by saying, "They have left their God to play the harlot." In other words, they have been unfaithful in wandering off after false gods. They have returned to the old ways by sacrificing "on the tops of mountains" and under oak trees "because their shade is good." (4:13)

In addition to this, even "brides commit adultery." This probably refers to rites occurring at Baal sanctuaries where the practice of sexual intercourse assured human fertility. But Hosea is no sexist. He says the men are no better: "The men themselves go aside with harlots, and sacrifice with cult prostitutes. . . ." (4:14) He believes that such harlotry will bring his people to ruin.

Hosea also refers to the actual physical making of idols: "With their silver and gold they made idols. . . ." (8:4) But he rejects the idea that any man can make God in the shape of a calf. He affirms: "A workman made it; it is not God. The calf of Samaria shall be broken to pieces." (8:6)

In another passage Hosea refers to the same practice. "Now they sin more and more, and make for themselves molten images, idols skillfully made of their silver." (13:2) Then scornfully he reproves them: "Sacrifice to these, they say. Men kiss calves!"

By such practices he sees his people bringing judgment upon themselves, coming to naught. In an especially poetic passage he says:

> Therefore, they shall be like the morning mist
> or like the dew that goes early away,
> like the chaff that swirls from the threshing floor
> or like smoke from a window. (13:3)

Or to put it another way: you will disappear.

Yet the people of Israel will never disappear from the face or the concern of their Lord. For, as Hosea declares with full confidence: God is wed to Israel despite her unfaithfulness.

In one of the most poignant passages in the book (11:1–4) Hosea describes God's attachment to Israel despite her rejection.

> When Israel was a child, I loved him,
>   and out of Egypt I called my son.
> The more I called them,
>   the more they went from me;
> they kept sacrificing to the Baals,
>   and burning incense to idols.

Yet, Hosea reminds them, Yahweh taught them to walk; he took them up in his arms and healed them. He was permanently *attached* to them with "cords of compassion" and "bands of love." He eased the yoke on their jaws. He bent down and fed them.

Still, as John Mauchline puts it so poetically, they did not respond: "In spite of the many evidences of God's love for his people, they were so blind and obtuse that they did not recognize his care and failed to trace the footprints of his ways."[3]

Further, Hosea makes clear that God wants love from his people rather than sacrifice. Ephraim, he declares, has made many altars of sacrifice for the purpose of taking away sin, yet these very altars have become "altars for sinning." (8:11) Israel has come to a state where

> They love sacrifice;
> they sacrifice flesh and eat it,
> but the LORD has no delight in them. (8:13)

They thought, erroneously, that if they went through the ritual, in some magical way that could take their sins away instead of expressing their devotion in positive acts of love. So obsessed were they that the religious law itself—the foundation of Hebrew religion—was being ignored: "Were I to write for him my laws by ten thousands, they would be regarded as a strange thing." (8:12) So offensive is this to the LORD that, as punishment, he is considering for them a "return to Egypt" from which bondage they had been delivered.

The prophet laments in the sixth chapter:

> What shall I do with you, O Ephraim?
> What shall I do with you, O Judah? (6:4a)

It is like a mother saying to an erring son, "What am I going to do with you!"

Then Hosea complains about Ephraim's shortlived love:

> Your love is like a morning cloud,
> like the dew that goes early away. (6:4b)

Because of this, through the prophets, God's judgment must go forth as the light. Then Hosea makes clear what the Lord really wants;

> For I desire steadfast love and not sacrifice,
> the knowledge of God, rather than burnt offerings. (6:6)

It is in this passage that the issue for the religion of Israel is succinctly joined. As Harold Cooke Phillips writes: "One confronts here the whole program of the relationship between ecclesiasticism and religion, between ritualism and righteousness, between symbol and substance; in short, between priestly and prophetic emphasis."[4]

The Lord wants "steadfast love" and not the sacrifice of flesh on the altar. As late as the time of Jesus, animal sacrifice was still taking place in the temple of Jerusalem. In Matthew 9:13 we find him quoting the previous passage from Hosea. The Pharisees had criticized Jesus for eating with tax collectors and sinners. When he heard that he said: " 'Those who are well have no need of a physician, but those who are sick. Go and learn what this means, "I desire mercy, and not sacrifice." For I came not to call the righteous but sinners.' " Thus Jesus used Hosea to elevate a truth which lay at the heart of his gospel.

In fact, a cursory review of the footnote references of the New Testament will reveal that its writers refer to the book of Hosea as much as any other prophetic book with the exception of Isaiah. The teachings of Hosea have many parallels in New Testament material.

HOSEA'S MESSAGE FOR THE MODERN ERA

One of the greatest lessons that Hosea has to teach contemporaries today concerns the *forgiving nature of God.* We find this coming through as Hosea reflects on his experience with his erring wife Gomer. He relates this to his feelings about the people of Israel. If he is willing to forgive Gomer and take her back to his bosom, so the Lord will forgive and restore Israel as his special people.

In the eleventh chapter, he declares God will not give up Ephraim or "hand over" Israel. He says:

> My heart recoils within me,
>   my compassion grows warm and tender.
> I will not execute my fierce anger . . .
> for I am God and not man . . .
>   and I will not come to destroy. (11:8, 9)

The normal nature of man is to lash out and destroy. But this is not the character of God. Although this was a hard lesson for Israel to learn, the prophet taught it. And if God is forgiving, then should not also men and women be forgiving?

So many persons, even devout Christians, do not really understand that God is forgiving. They are shackled with guilt. Because they feel so anxious about their guilt, they considerably reduce their effectiveness. They feel inferior because they think they should always be punished and never rewarded. They find it hard to accept a complimentary word or a gift with grace. They may think people don't like them—because, in their own estimation, they are unworthy. Worse than this, they project their guilt; they may accuse others of the thing they feel guilty about. A husband may accuse a wife of infidelity because he has been unfaithful. A mother may accuse her daughter of promiscuity because she herself entertains unclean thoughts. A father may accuse his son of lying because he has done so under similar circumstances.

Who knows how many wars have been started because some national leader felt miserable and expressed his or her guilt through paranoia against a neighboring nation? Who knows how many crimes have been committed because the perpetrators felt guilty and actually wanted to get caught for doing something terrible? Who knows how many "accident prone" people cause serious accidents because they feel that justice calls for punishing themselves?

But Hosea was saying, "You don't have to go around weighted down and destroyed by all that guilt. Know the truth: that the Lord is a forgiving God and he will set you free." So men and women don't have to walk though life stooped over. They don't have to look away when you look them in the eye. They don't have to apologize for living. They don't have to project the unworthiness which they feel themselves. They can be human because God is God and not a man or woman. They can walk tall in the full freedom of forgiven persons.

Another cue we can take from Hosea's words almost 3000 years old is *not to trust in military power.* Many of the prophets reflected this, of course. It is more tempting for the United States, a large and economically powerful country, to fall victim to such misplaced trust than tiny Israel, whose resources were extremely limited. Yet the lesson still applies.

Hosea makes his point clearly:

> Because you have trusted in your chariots
>   and in the multitude of your warriors,
> therefore the tumult of war shall arise among your people,
>   and all your fortresses shall be destroyed.(10:13b-14a)

The United States is the greatest military power on earth. At this writing it has an authorized defense budget of $112.1 billion, including foreign military aid and nuclear weapons.

Why do we "trust in chariots" so much? Actually there are limits to what military power can do. With all our armed might, we don't seem to be able to prevent the existence of a communist Cuba only about 90 miles off the Florida coast. Nor is there any strong sentiment for using our overkill to wipe out the bastion of our adversary, the Soviet Union. Actually, other kinds of power, ethical and economic, are often more usable than military power in certain situations.

Trusting in chariots has not enhanced freedom in South America. Now, regrettably, out of the ten major countries of that continent, all but two are under the control of military dictatorships. Juntas were enabled to take control of the governments of Chile, Uruguay, and Argentina in recent years with arms provided largely through U.S. military aid. In each of these countries the new regimes have been very oppressive. In formerly democratic Chile, the takeover was implemented through a bloody coup with President Allende being shot to death. In Uruguay the government has incarcerated more political prisoners, on a basis of percentage of population, than in any other South American country. In Argentina the military junta permits right-wing para-police squads to roam the cities and dispense vigilante justice. As a result, more people have been killed in one year in Argentina than in five years in Northern Ireland.

U.S. arms and training of South American military officers have been used, not to defend the neighboring continent against outside attack, but to oppress, subjugate, and terrorize their own people.

Not only the United States stands under judgment for "trusting in chariots." An entire world trend in this direction is now apparent. A recent report entitled *World Military and Social Expenditures 1976* sets forth these startling facts.[5] Close to $300 billion in public funds are being spent annually on armaments. As the report points out: "It is destructive, whether or not the weapons are put to use in war. It contributes to inflation, retards economic and social development, and diverts resources urgently needed for human well-being. Until it can be put under control, it undermines the national and international security which it is intended to protect."[6]

The report indicates that governments of developing countries are spending as much on military programs as they are on education and health combined. But the developed nations are also at fault; the richer countries are spending more for the military than for the economic development of the poorer countries. World military expenditures average $12,330 per soldier while public expenditures for education are approximately $219 per school-age child. The expenditures report reveals that, in fifteen years, military spending in developing countries more than doubled from $15 billion in 1960 to $39 billion in 1974 (in constant 1973 dollars).

Even though nuclear weapons have not been used in thirty years, expenditures for them account for about one fifth of the world's military costs. Since 1945 when there were only two strategic nuclear weapons, the number has grown to over 12,000 at present. And the smallest of these is three times larger than the Hiroshima bomb. It is almost impossible to comprehend the explosive force of current nuclear power. As the report states: "A single bomber today can carry a warload equivalent to 10 million tons of TNT, about twice the tonnage released by all combatants in World War II. The nuclear stockpiles of the two superpowers alone contain the equivalent in destructive power of 1,300,000 Hiroshima-size bombs. They represent a powder keg of tons of explosives for every man, woman and child on earth."[7]

What "trusting in chariots" means to human needs worldwide becomes frighteningly apparent. In the developing countries governments are spending less than one-fourth as much on health as on their military programs. Worldwide, about half as much is spent on health care as on the military. Three dollars per capita is spent by governments of developing countries compared to $134 per capita by developed nations. In relation to population there are 3 physicians and 13 hospital beds per 10,000 people in the developing areas and 19 doctors and 100 beds per 10,000 in the developed areas.

For the ten-year war against small pox, which was expected to eradicate the disease by 1976, the World Health Organization set a budget of $250 million. Yet the world has been spending more than that on military programs in eight hours.

Spiraling outlays for arms have a hidden cost: the inadequately financed social programs that cannot meet human needs.

Another value we may glean from Hosea is his focus upon *the grace of God.* Confronted with the apostasy of Israel, Hosea is moved to say "What shall I do with you?" (6:4) So full of iniquity is Ephraim that Hosea pictures God as saying: "Compassion is hid from my eyes." (13:14) But this is shortlived. The natural response of God is to exercise grace, "the undeserved love of God."

Hosea reflects this in a lovely passage in the last chapter. On behalf of the Lord he proclaims:

> I will heal their faithlessness;
>> I will love them freely,
>> for my anger has turned from them.
> I will be as the dew to Israel;
>> he shall blossom as the lily,
>> he shall strike roots as the poplar;
> his shoots shall spread out;
>> his beauty shall be like the olive,
>> and his fragrance like Lebanon.
> They shall return and dwell beneath my shadow,
>> they shall flourish as a garden;
> they shall blossom as the vine;
>> their fragrance shall be like [Lebanon's wine]. (14:4–7)

Hosea says, "I will be as the dew to Israel"—for as the dew refreshes the earth, so God's grace refreshes the spirit.

A fine woman of Lutheran background once told me that as a child she was taught to "look for grace." Too often in our lives we are looking for trouble, looking for slights or offense, looking for something to gossip about, looking for revenge. But grace is there if we will look for it. We find it in a child gathering a bouquet of violets for a visiting relative, in a friend doing us an unexpected favor, in a healing that comes to a body we have abused.

We find it in nature—in the sweet song of a joyous cardinal in May, in the energetic flight of squirrels among high branches of leafless wintry trees. We find it in the subtle fragrance of flowering spring, in the kaleidoscopic colors of autumn, the soft embrace of a warm summer breeze.

Our nation has also enjoyed the blessing of the grace of God. We have a temperate climate, expansive forests, abundant natural resources, bumper grain crops, and an extensive continental shelf under which lie huge stores of oil. Favored with oceans on either side that provide a natural defense, and friendly nations to both the north and south, the United States stands in an enviable position to maintain her peace.

Grace is the undeserved love of God; that's the way God operates. But we are easily led into the trap of talking about the "deserving poor," or that some nations are more deserving than others. Those persons we consider more "deserving" are often the more industrious, those who will lift a finger to help themselves, or those who have an excuse for their poverty, like a widow with three young children. But the person who is born mentally handicapped, or the family caught in the cycle of poverty, or the persons who have given up on hunting for jobs because they have been turned down so often—it may be hard to think of them as "deserving."

But when it comes right down to it, who is deserving of God's grace? That is, who besides you and me?

Our role as Christians is to be "ministers of grace"—to look where the hurt is and help heal it, to look where the anger and bitterness are and absorb it, to look for people who need love: the hostile, the dispossessed, the exploited, those discriminated against, those powerless to help themselves. Some city churches try to do this by initiating a "shepherds of the streets" program. Clergy and lay persons trained in counseling and helpful referral services make themselves available on city streets late at night when ordinary people are asleep. They often minister to the so-called "undeserving," the drunks, prostitutes, pick-pockets, and derelicts.

One person who became a minister of grace was Sir Wilfred Grenfell. Trained as a physician, he entered the service of the Royal National Mission to Deep Sea Fishermen and sailed to Iceland in 1889. Later, with hospital supplies, he was sent to explore living conditions among the people of Labrador and Newfoundland. He found many suffering from beriberi and tuberculosis with no doctors to help. Within three months he treated 900 patients. For the next forty years he served the people of that region, helping to establish hospitals, orphanages, schools and cooperative stores in the cold, bleak terrain near the Arctic Circle. At the time of his death, friends discovered that, to guide him in his ministry to marginal and forgotten people, he had affixed these words to the inside top of his medicine bag: "Be kinder than necessary."

It was out of Hosea's experience with his wife Gomer that he projected his reflections upon the nation of Israel. Gomer had been unfaithful, left her husband, and become a prostitute. Yet Hosea took her back into his household and his heart. He found he could do this, not out of a sense of obligation, but out of the overflow of God's love for him.

If America is to be a blessing to the nations, it will be because she *wants* to, not because she *has* to, in response to those good gifts that God in his gracious benevolence has showered upon us. It will be because Americans are moved to be "ministers of grace," to share their harvests and their technology, to share their idealistic youth, and to share even in the risks of a disarming world. In this way the kingdom of God could come, moving out from within our hearts, blessed by grace to bless mankind.

Selections from Hosea

PLAYING THE HARLOT 2:2–7

"Plead with your mother, plead—
  for she is not my wife,
  and I am not her husband—
that she put away her harlotry from her face,
  and her adultery from between her breasts;
lest I strip her naked
  and make her as in the day she was born,
and make her like a wilderness,
  and set her like a parched land, and slay her with thirst.
Upon her children also I will have no pity,
  because they are children of harlotry.
For their mother has played the harlot;
  she that conceived them has acted shamefully.
For she said, 'I will go after my lovers,
  who give me my bread and my water,
  my wool and my flax, my oil and my drink.'
Therefore I will hedge up her way with thorns;
  and I will build a wall against her, so that she cannot find her paths.
She shall pursue her lovers,
  but not overtake them,
and she shall seek them,
  but shall not find them.
Then she shall say, 'I will go
  and return to my first husband,
  for it was better with me then than now.' "

BUYING BACK A LOVER 3:1–3

And the Lord said to me, "Go again, love a woman who is beloved of a paramour and is an adulteress; even as the LORD loves the people of Israel, though they turn to other gods and love cakes of raisins." So I bought her for fifteen shekels of silver and a homer and a lethech of barley. And I said to her, "You must dwell as mine for many days; you shall not play the harlot, or belong to another man; so will I also be to you."

THE LORD HAS A CONTROVERSY WITH HIS PEOPLE 4:1–3

Hear the word of the LORD, O people of Israel;
    for the LORD has a controversy with the inhabitants of the land.
There is no faithfulness or kindness,
    and no knowledge of God in the land;
there is swearing, lying, killing, stealing, and committing adultery;
    they break all bounds and murder follows murder.
        Therefore the land mourns,
        and all who dwell in it languish,
and also the beasts of the field,
    and the birds of the air;
    and even the fish of the sea are taken away.

A PEOPLE WITHOUT UNDERSTANDING 4:11–14

Wine and new wine
    take away the understanding.
My people inquire of a thing of wood,
    and their staff gives them oracles.
For a spirit of harlotry has led them astray,
    and they have left their God to play the harlot.
They sacrifice on the tops of the mountains,
    and make offerings upon the hills,
under oak, poplar, and terebinth,
    because their shade is good.
Therefore your daughters play the harlot,
    and your brides commit adultery.
I will not punish your daughters when they play the harlot,
    nor your brides when they commit adultery;
for the men themselves go aside with harlots,
    and sacrifice with cult prostitutes,
and a people without understanding shall come to ruin.

WHAT SHALL I DO WITH YOU? 6:1–6

"Come, let us return to the LORD;
    for he has torn, that he may heal us;
    he has stricken, and he will bind us up.
After two days he will revive us;
    on the third day he will raise us up,
    that we may live before him.
Let us know, let us press on to know the LORD;
    his going forth is sure as the dawn;

he will come to us as the showers,
   as the spring rains that water the earth."
What shall I do with you, O Ephraim?
   What shall I do with you, O Judah?
Your love is like a morning cloud,
   like the dew that goes early away.
Therefore I have hewn them by the prophets,
   I have slain them by the words of my mouth,
   and my judgment goes forth as the light.
For I desire steadfast love and not sacrifice,
   the knowledge of God, rather than burnt offerings.

REAP THE WHIRLWIND 8:1–8

Set the trumpet to your lips,
   for a vulture is over the house of the LORD,
because they have broken my covenant,
   and transgressed my law.
To me they cry,
   My God, we Israel know thee.
Israel has spurned the good;
   the enemy shall pursue him.
They made kings, but not through me.
   They set up princes, but without my knowledge.
With their silver and gold they made idols
   for their own destruction.
I have spurned your calf, O Samaria.
   My anger burns against them.
How long will it be
   till they are pure in Israel?
A workman made it;
   it is not God.
The calf of Samaria
   shall be broken to pieces.
For they sow the wind,
   and they shall reap the whirlwind.
The standing grain has no heads,
   it shall yield no meal;
if it were to yield,
   aliens would devour it.
Israel is swallowed up;
   already they are among the nations
   as a useless vessel.

ALTARS FOR SINNING 8:11–13

Because Ephraim has multiplied altars for sinning,
   they have become to him altars for sinning.
Were I to write for him my laws by ten thousands,
   they would be regarded as a strange thing.
They love sacrifice;
   they sacrifice flesh and eat it;
   but the Lord has no delight in them.
Now he will remember their iniquity,
   and punish their sins. . . .

TRUSTING IN CHARIOTS 10:12–14a

Sow for yourselves righteousness,
   reap the fruit of steadfast love;
   break up your fallow ground,
for it is the time to seek the LORD,
   that he may come and rain salvation upon you.
You have plowed iniquity,
   you have reaped injustice,
   you have eaten the fruit of lies.
Because you have trusted in your chariots
   and in the multitude of your warriors,
therefore the tumult of war shall arise among your people,
   and all your fortresses shall be destroyed. . . .

WITH CORDS OF COMPASSION 11:1–4

When Israel was a child, I loved him,
   and out of Egypt I called my son.
The more I called them,
   the more they went from me;
they kept sacrificing to the Baals,
   and burning incense to idols.
Yet it was I who taught Ephraim to walk,
   I took them up in my arms;
   but they did not know that I healed them.
I led them with cords of compassion,
   with the bands of love,
and I became to them as one
   who eases the yoke on their jaws,
   and I bent down to them and fed them.

I AM GOD, NOT MAN 11:8, 9

How can I give you up, O Ephraim!
　　How can I hand you over, O Israel!
How can I make you like Admah!
　　How can I treat you like Zeboiim!
My heart recoils within me,
　　my compassion grows warm and tender.
I will not execute my fierce anger,
　　I will not again destroy Ephraim;
for I am God and not man,
　　the Holy One in your midst,
　　and I will not come to destroy.

SACRIFICE LEADS TO NAUGHT 13:1–3

When Ephraim spoke, men trembled;
　　he was exalted in Israel;
　　but he incurred guilt through Baal and died.
And now they sin more and more
　　and make for themselves molten images,
idols skilfully made of their silver,
　　all of them the work of craftsmen.
Sacrifice to these, they say.
　　Men kiss calves!
Therefore they shall be like the morning mist
　　or like the dew that goes early away,
like the chaff that swirls from the threshing floor
　　or like smoke from a window.

I WILL LOVE THEM FREELY 14:4–9

I will heal their faithlessness;
　　I will love them freely,
　　for my anger has turned from them.
I will be as the dew to Israel;
　　he shall blossom as the lily,
　　he shall strike root as the poplar;
his shoots shall spread out;
　　his beauty shall be like the olive,
　　and his fragrance like Lebanon.
They shall return and dwell beneath my shadow,
　　they shall flourish as a garden;
they shall blossom as the vine,

their fragrance shall be like the wine of Lebanon.
O Ephraim, what have I to do with idols?
    It is I who answer and look after you.
I am like an evergreen cypress,
    from me comes your fruit.
Whoever is wise, let him understand these things;
    whoever is discerning, let him know them;
for the ways of the LORD are right,
    and the upright walk in them,
    but transgressors stumble in them.

Hosea—Prophet of Forgiving Love

THE PEOPLE OF AMERICA (3:1)

The Lord loves the people of America
  though they turn to other gods.
Though they politick with one another
  to place themselves in positions of power
  and forget wherein true power lies;
though they achieve self-assurance by accumulating wealth,
  and deny the self-worth of those poor
  who have a good reputation;
though they are obsessed with slot machines and gaming tables
  and will surrender all before compulsion ebbs;
though they amass their bombs
  and do not serve as a balm to troubled peoples in poverty;
though they have made a religion of anti-communism
  and base their faith on fear and hate;
though they feed their vanity
  and let the poor beg for food;
or frequent the watering places
  while the thirsty gather at dry wells;
the Lord loves the people of [America]
  and believes they will turn again to him.

CRIME (4:1, 2)

Hear the word of the Lord, O people of America;
  for the Lord has a controversy with the inhabitants of the land.
There is no faithfulness or kindness,
  and no knowledge of God in the land;
there is swearing, lying, killing, stealing, and committing adultery. . . .
Why are people so set against one another?
Why are they willing to exploit, even destroy, one another?
Why is there no sense of community?
Why do people feel they don't belong to anything, to anyone?
People will not lie—
  if they feel they are disgracing their own beloved society.
Persons will not steal—

if they know they are robbing their own people.
No one will be moved to murder—
  in a society where they know they are loved.
So, recognize your humanness,
  that you are bound together as children of God,
  and watch over one another in the spirit of love.
Let no man be an outsider,
  no woman be a loner, no child be introverted,
  no person without community.
Let each person feel cared for, that he or she belongs, has roots,
  and a chance to flower.

GUN VIOLENCE (4:2)

Woe unto you, ordinary citizens!
For you are being shot by one another three times as often as
    by criminals.
[You] *break all bounds and murder follows murder.*
And more of you were killed at home by handguns during the
    Vietnam war than were destroyed abroad in that terrible conflict.
You buy guns for home protection, and end by shooting a
    loved one, a friend, or neighbor.
Or your home is burglarized when you are not at home,
  and the thief steals the handgun which was supposed to protect
    your domicile.
Wake up, Americans!
You are turning your nation into a no-man's land.
Husbands are killing wives in moments of unreasoned rage.
Children are shooting neighbors with guns they treat as toys.
Youth gangs are attacking one another with pistols instead of bare fists.
Seven-Elevens are robbed routinely
  and the police are not safe on their beats.
You deceive yourselves into thinking
  there's some God-given right to bear arms,
  a right which, if claimed for yourself, must also be extended
    to every felon, every drug addict, every alcoholic,
    depressed, or paranoid person.
You affirm that sentencing criminals to long terms
  will deter them from violence,
  when most do not even get caught!
You say that "guns don't kill people,"
Yet in Britain where guns are not easily available

the gun murder rate is 100 times less than ours.
Away with your Second Amendment myth,
   your pat slogans that are patently false,
   your legislative tricks,
   your claims that the "armed citizen" always survives in gun play.
Let common sense hold sway:
   turn in your handguns for the common good,
   turn back the violence and the shedding of human blood,
   and receive your compensation
      in streets that are safer for citizens to walk;
      in crime rates that begin to level off,
      in persons who are alive and not statistics,
      in a society seeking to be civilized.

UNDERSTANDING (4:14)

A people without understanding shall come to ruin.
If you don't understand that gun crime is related to the availability of
    guns,
if you can't understand that the death penalty is largely reserved for the
    poor, the blacks, and the powerless,
if you don't understand that inflation cannot be forever combatted by
    creating joblessness,
then may the LORD have mercy on your soul.
If you don't understand that welfare mothers are not going to take jobs
    unless they are provided with decent child care,
if you don't understand that busing children wouldn't be necessary if
    housing patterns were integrated,
if you don't understand that Vietnam war objectors in exile wondered
    why the U.S. warmly accepted Vietnamese refugees while American
    citizens who opposed the war were ostracized,
if you don't understand that Panamanians resent the U.S. ruling their
    territory with "extra-territorial rights,"
if you don't understand why black Zimbabwe resists being governed by
    a minority of white Rhodesians,
if you don't understand that black South Africans will not forever endure
    being told where they must live, what jobs they may hold, what wages
    they may receive, how little power they may exert on the
    government,
      then may God have mercy on your soul.
If you don't understand that wiretapping makes people afraid to share
    their thoughts, and thus limits free speech,

if you don't understand that nuclear energy creates long-lived poisonous
    wastes, for which scientific ingenuity has not yet been able to develop
    safe storage,
if you don't understand that high defense expenditures
  which pay for weapons soon obsolete
  are a highly inflationary factor in our economy,
    because people are using their productive power to create
    nonconsumable goods,
        then may God have mercy on your soul,
        and spare the Nation from the ruin of its folly.

NUCLEAR ENERGY (8:7)

They sow the wind,
  and they shall reap the whirlwind.
You build your nuclear plants because you expect
  someday to run out of oil.
Yet you have coal reserves to last
  for hundreds of years,
  and a sun that will outlive mankind.
You expand your nuclear power program
  even though you are not sure
  the safety systems will work.
The power industry assures the public:
  "You are protected!"
  "You are protected!"
but they refuse to bear the full risk
  in case of accident.
Nuclear planners expect five hundred operating plants
  by the end of the century.
So you have planned the technology;
  have you also planned for the well-being of humanity?
Since plants have already been closed down
  because of accidents,
how will you guarantee the risk
  of building ten times the number of reactors?
Or, again—how can you be sure that plutonium—
  the most poisonous substance on earth,
  with a half-life of over 24,000 years—
  can be transported safely?
What about the drum of nuclear fuel
  which fell off the truck in Connecticut?
What if it had spilled open

and laid waste the land and the people?
We already know what kepone can do;
 we don't want to discover firsthand
 the deadliness of nuclear poison.
How have you protected us against terrorist attack?
You have assured us that trucks transporting fuel
 will be accompanied by an armored vehicle
 and several armed guards.
But could not a desperate band, willing to take the risk,
 still capture the powerful and dangerous fuel
 and blackmail humanity?
You have sown the wind,
 and we may reap the whirlwind.
Again, you have smoothed our brows
 and tranquilized our anxious spirits
 by assuring us that nuclear wastes
 can be stored in old salt mines
 located in stable parts of the country.
With an increasing number of earthquakes
 occurring where they never occurred before,
 where is the "stable area"?
Is there any location on earth
 where you can guarantee no quake?
 no seepage of fatal fuel wastes
 into the underground waters some will drink?
 or above ground air that some may breathe?
You talk of sharing nuclear plants abroad
 with adequate safeguards,
but how can you impose safeguards on other countries
 when in your own nation
 your people are far from "safe"?
If, as your experts have said,
 thirty-five countries
 may have nuclear plants
 that could make bombs by 1985,
 why, by your example, do you keep sowing the wind?

VIETNAM—LOOKING BACK (10:13, 14)

You have plowed iniquity,
 You have reaped injustice.
You sprayed their vegetation with defoliate
 and failed to help the people grow their crops.

You propped up in office a bunch of ruthless dictators
  and issued another press release about defending the bastion of
    freedom.
You have eaten the fruit of lies:
so often did your public relations office put out optimistic progress
    reports
that your generals began to believe that they were true.
You have trusted in your air power
and in the multitude of your armed battalions,
  but they were not enough.
For you did not know the terrain, the climate, the language or culture,
and so you were an alien people fighting in a foreign land.
You trusted in armed might, but not in elections.
You trusted leaders with a familiar religion,
  but not the Buddhists backed by most of the people.
You used B-52 bombers to combat "warriors" armed with bamboo sticks.
You herded peasants into refugee camps
and destroyed villages in order to "save" villagers.
But the villagers did not want to be saved
and the peasants wanted only to live in peace, and till their own ancestral
    lands.
You thought that massive numbers of outside troops
could easily defeat little bands of indigenous rebels living close to the
    earth.
You were wrong,
but you wouldn't admit it.
Your leaders returned saying: "We've turned the corner!"
  or "The troops will be home for Christmas!"
For you were taken in by your own news releases,
but you could not read the signs of the times.
You turned the people who produced the rice bowl of Asia
  into millions of refugees with empty bowls begging for food.
You spent thirty billion a year on a futile foreign war,
  while at home you could not afford low income housing, decent health
      care, or food stamps for the hungry poor.
There would have been no war in Vietnam if you had not intervened with
    massive support for a puppet regime.
You were not on the wrong side:
  you *were* the wrong side.
You placed nails in the coffins of children
  by spraying poison over the foliage they ate.
You said that for Orientals, life was cheap.

Then you "proved" it
  by wiping out their dwelling places
  massacring their My Lais
  and carpet bombing their cities.
Through your bloodshot eyes,
  all Vietnamese looked like "Gooks,"
and so you could
  skin their children alive with napalm bombs
  burn holes in their flesh with phosphorus explosives
  and let allies pour lye on them in tiger cages.
You were like the Germans near Dachau:
  you really didn't know
    your nation's brutalities to other human beings. . . .
Or did you prefer not to know?
You thought you were strengthening the "free world,"
  but stifled dissent in your own country.
You thought you were supporting international law,
  but did not implement elections under the Geneva Accords.
You thought you were combatting atheistic communism
  by putting Christians into power
  though most Vietnamese were followers of Buddha.
You thought the war would be a short one
  through applying massive force,
but forgot the tactics of Washington
  against well-trained British troops.
You thought you were saving the people
  by putting the torch to their huts,
but your scorched earth policies made the people you were "defending"
    burn with resentment.
Therefore, the tumult of war shall arise among your [own] *people*
  and all your fortresses shall be destroyed.

THE BLESSED AMERICA (14:4–6)

I will heal their faithlessness;
  I will love them freely,
    for my anger has turned from them.
I will be as the dew to America;
  it shall blossom as the lily,
  it shall strike root as the forsythia;
its shoots shall spread out;
  its beauty shall be like the apple
  and its fragrance like redwood.

So children shall be born in wholeness,
  and the elderly die in dignity.
And in-between you shall live
  a rich and useful life.
For in that day
  you shall see no trash on the street,
  pick up no gum on your shoes;
nature's view will be unobstructed
  by gaudy billboards.
Petty crime offenders
  will be loved back into the community,
and the mentally ill who withdraw
  will re-enter a society
    pleasant enough to return to.
The cackle of gossip over back fences
  has turned into words of warm praise,
  and many fences have come down.
Newcomers are welcomed with grace
  and old-timers held in high esteem,
and all enjoy belonging
  to recognized communities.
Persons save their unrenewable resources,
  pollute not the air,
    nor muddy the waters.
Instead, they replenish the earth
  with natural fertilizers
    and nitrogen-absorbing plants.
And so air and water and earth
  are inherited by future generations
    as their rich legacy.
Those who work have meaningful jobs,
  and those who cannot labor
    are sustained,
and no one is made to feel
  a burden to society.
The teeth of every child are attended
  and persons don't reach adulthood
    wearing dentures the rest of their lives.
Doctors are paid to keep people well
  and hospitals used for serious illness
    and emergency care.
Children grow up asking for fruit

and not for candy bars,
and junk food is not dispensed from
vending machines.
Builders construct houses to last
and slums are forgotten memories
of the past.
Residents enjoy their open spaces
and pleasant parks,
convenient public transportation
and nearby shops.
And no one is forced to live
in rat-infested, dilapidated
dungeons of hell.
Cities are marvelous places to live
and the countryside a healing balm. . . .
And I will not melt you down
into one nondescript blob;
but I will let you be yourselves:
so blacks study history
and rejoice in their roots,
and Chicanos bake their tasty tortillas.
The Jewish people celebrate their Passover
and the Poles dance a merry polka.
The Swedes honor their candle-crowned queen
of Saint Lucia,
and Puerto Ricans celebrate their
joyous fiestas.
The Amish trot their buggies along
a dusty road,
and Indians preserve sacred rites
on native lands.
And no one is forced to be the same
for cultural diversity reigns supreme.
For I shall be to you as dew in the morning
as a warm fresh breeze at midday
and a glorious scarlet sky at dusk,
as that day comes
when you watch over one another in love
and all humanity
is your extended family.

III | FIRST ISAIAH

HIS TIMES AND OURS

*This indicates new material in this edition

The New American Isolationism
The Wolf with the Lamb (11:9, 6)
A Tale of Two Cities (13—19)
The Free World (21—23)
Separation—White from Black
Communism
"The Spirit Giveth Life" (28:13)
Barren Plans and Alliances (30:1-2)
The Circle of Death (30:12, 13)
Response to God's Grace (30:15, 18)
Woe to Those— (31)
*Feeding the Hungry (32:6)
*Women's Rights (32:9, 11)
The Pleasant Little War
*The Death Penalty (Excerpts from Isaiah 38)
The Russian Orthodox Church
The Control of Power
By Whose Principles?
The Gift of Peace

First Isaiah—His Times and Ours

Isaiah, the eighth-century prophet of Jerusalem, differed from most other major prophetic figures in serving as a political advisor at the highest level—a confidant of kings. Well educated and undoubtedly steeped in religious training, he was of a nobleman's family and thus had access to the royal court. Of this special privilege he took utmost advantage. Highly respected, he seems to have held the king's ear even when he voiced unpopular opinions and counsel.

HISTORICAL BACKGROUND

The author of chapters 1–39 of Isaiah is often called First Isaiah so as to distinguish him from the writer of chapters 40–66 who lived in a later period. The public life of First Isaiah spanned some forty years of a most difficult period in Hebrew history. The dominant world power was Assyria to the northeast. Tiny Judah was alternately trapped and pushed by three forces—a desire for independence, the temptation to join alliances to enhance her security, and the constant threat of subjugation or assimilation by the powerful Assyrian kingdom. Invading armies periodically marched into Judah. Her immediate neighbor to the north, the kingdom of Israel, eventually disappeared with the siege and fall of Samaria.

The prophet Isaiah served in this environment as spokesman for God. Beginning his prophetic activity as a young man in the year of the death of King Uzziah, who ruled from 783 to 742 B.C., Isaiah continued his work during the reign of three other kings of Judah from 742 to 687 B.C.: Jotham, Ahaz, and Hezekiah.

The prophet received his call "in the year that King Uzziah died." Uzziah's successful reign had been marked by peace and prosperity. As far as the people were concerned it was not "time for a change." But change came, and with it great anxiety about the future. For during that very year, Tiglath-pileser III of Assyria invaded northern Israel and exacted a heavy tribute.

Sitting in the temple one day, brooding over the situation that confronted his unhappy land, Isaiah had a deep religious experience (6:1–8). He was overwhelmed by a sense of the holiness of God—a holiness which by comparison made him feel like "a man of unclean lips" dwelling "in the midst of a people of unclean lips." Holiness in early Old Testament times had denoted largely the separateness and aloofness of God without any moral overtones. Isaiah sees God's holiness in the fullness of its ethical richness. It is in the presence of this kind of God that he senses his own unworthiness.

Then a voice from heaven speaks to his anxious soul, "Your guilt is taken away, and your sin forgiven." When the voice of the Lord says, "Who will go for us?" Isaiah becomes conscious of the great need of his people for redemption and for restored faith in a God who is himself holy and who expects holiness of his people. With such an awareness of the awesome task to which he is called, Isaiah accepts his commission as a prophet.

WHAT SORT OF MAN WAS ISAIAH?

Despite Isaiah's education, nobility, and ready access to the royal court, Judah's rulers were inclined more often than not to ignore his advice.

Although he might have had reason, by virtue of background, to remain aloof as part of the socially elite, he was primarily an aristocrat of the spirit. Equally at home with kings and commoners, he spoke with the dignity and authority of one who knew he was under divine command.

Married and the father of two children, Isaiah was apparently a devoted family man. He referred to his wife as "the prophetess" and gave his children names which witnessed to his own prophetic message.

THE MAJOR TEACHINGS OF ISAIAH

To Isaiah, insatiable greed, drunken debauchery, and indifference to the predicament of the poor reflected a serious condition—rejection of the will of God, whose character is basically ethical. Isaiah is deeply concerned that "the faithful city has become a harlot." He is appalled by the shallow vanity of the haughty young women of the day "mincing along as they go." He calls into question those whose primary concern in life is avariciously to "join house to house." The political leader who "loves a bribe and runs after gifts" comes under his lashing. Those who "rise early in the morning" to "run after strong drink" are denounced by Isaiah's fiery tongue.

Isaiah is nauseated by meaningless religious rites—burnt offerings, the multiplication of "new moons" and "appointed feasts," the spreading forth of hands, and the mouthing of long prayers. Instead the Lord God wants goodness, justice, relief for the oppressed, and compassion for the helpless and distressed.

THE PROPHET AS POLITICAL COUNSELOR

Since Isaiah found that relatively few heeded his words, he began to despair of the masses turning from their evil ways. However, he felt that sooner or later a creative minority would begin to understand what God wanted. These would in time become the leaven in the lump, renewing in mankind a more dedicated devotion to the will of the Lord. As a result of this faith, Isaiah named his first-born son "Shear-jashub," which literally means "a remnant shall return."

In 735 B.C. the kingdoms of Israel and Syria to the north joined forces to remove themselves from the threat of complete domination by Assyria. To strengthen their cause they called upon Judah to participate in a mutual assistance pact. When Judah's king, Ahaz, refused the offer, preferring neutrality, these two states moved upon Judah in an attempt to force her to become a part of the alliance. They took a position not without parallel in our contemporary era: "To be my friend you must be the enemy of my enemy." Under these circumstances King Ahaz was greatly tempted to call upon Assyria for protection.

During this emergency situation, Isaiah, taking Shear-jashub with him, went to counsel with the king. He found Ahaz out inspecting the city's water supply—a resource of the greatest importance should Jerusalem become besieged. Referring to Syria and Israel, Isaiah admonished Judah: "Take heed, be quiet, do not fear, and do not let your heart be faint because of these two smoldering stumps of firebrands." (7:4) Isaiah encouraged the king to place his faith in the security that God would provide him if he led his nation in the paths of righteousness. If Judah instead depended upon Assyria for safety, she was doomed.

Perhaps one can appreciate the boldness of Isaiah's act if he imagines a respected national leader visiting the President during the height of the Cuban crisis, cautioning against rash action and recommending that he place his faith in righteous conduct. Then he might add: "By the way, Mr. President, this is my son 'Somebody-Shall-Be-Left' "!

To make his message even more striking, Isaiah named his next son "Maher-shalal-hash-baz" ("speeding to the spoil, hastening to the prey"). Those who think preachers' children are handicapped should reserve their pity for prophets' progeny!

Nevertheless Isaiah's warning went unheeded. Ahaz chose to send emissaries to the Assyrian king, Tiglath-pileser, pledging homage in exchange for Judah's defense. Gold and silver from the temple and palace accompanied the king's ambassadors as a persuasive tribute. Revelation of the plotted revolt against Assyria was all the excuse that Tiglath-pileser needed to march into northern Israel in 734 B.C., occupying the territory east of the Jordan and reducing the rest of the kingdom to a tiny Assyrian vassal. Two years later Syria also was defeated with the capture of Damascus. In 721 B.C. the Northern Kingdom went out of existence and became an Assyrian province.

Thus Judah's position was little improved as a result of the bargain she made. She lost two buffer states between herself and the major power of the day; she was now under the suzerainty of Assyria to whom she had to pay an annual tribute; and to make matters worse she fell under the corrupting influence of Assyrian religion. Ahaz even went so far as to install in the holy temple at Jerusalem a pagan altar modeled after a similar Assyrian piece he had admired on a trip to Damascus.

At this turn of events, Isaiah disgustedly went into seclusion with his family and a few disciples. He was out of public view during the balance of the reign of Ahaz.

Shortly after Hezekiah's ascendancy to the throne, Judah was again faced with a difficult choice. The cities of Philistia, prodded by Egypt and Ethiopia, attempted to free themselves from Sargon II, then the Assyrian monarch. In doing so, they sought support from Judah. Isaiah was strongly opposed to Judah's joining the alliance, and to dramatically demonstrate his objection, he walked naked for three years about the city of Jerusalem. This was to warn his fellow citizens that they would become captives and slaves if they took part in the revolt. No doubt Isaiah's behavior was an embarrassment to government officials as well as to his countrymen, just as today when demonstrators march with placards for peace or racial justice, those in power may be embarrassed and passersby may wish to dissociate themselves from "those radicals."

Isaiah was convinced that Assyria in time would be overthrown. Judah, he felt, should submit to Assyrian rule quietly and trustfully, waiting for that time when God, the Ruler of history, would act to deliver her from oppression. Therefore, the prophet denounced the leaders of Judah who "go down to Egypt for help" and "who trust in chariots." Instead should they not "look to the Holy One of Israel" and "consult the Lord"?

Like the first President of the United States, Isaiah seems to be warning against "entangling alliances" which may in themselves offer no security but instead involve a nation unnecessarily in adventures not in her own interest. G. G. D. Kilpatrick interprets Isaiah as saying here: " 'The truth is that God is the Lord of history, and until you recognize that, until you believe that his power is greater than man's, and that the defeat of the enemies of his purpose is his concern, your clever diplomacy is futile.' "[1] In this instance Hezekiah accepted the advice of Isaiah. Thus, when the commander-in-chief of Sargon "came to Ashdod and fought against it and took it," Judah was spared.

However, the death of Sargon II in 705 B.C. gave the signal to the restless cities of Babylonia and Philistia, supported by Egypt, to make a concerted attempt to throw off the yoke of Assyria. Conceding to Babylonian overtures, King Hezekiah unfortunately agreed to join the rebellion.

Sennacherib, now king of Assyria, marched southward in 701 B.C. to smash the revolt. Following a siege he took the Judean city of Lachish and made it into his new base for operations against King Hezekiah.

At this point Isaiah began to look upon Assyria as the rod of God's anger—the means by which the Lord was exercising his judgment against Judah for her perverseness. Isaiah did not mean to imply that Assyria's behavior was approved by God, for she herself would be punished in due time. But meanwhile God would make use of Assyria to discipline his wayward child Judah. For God was indeed the Lord of all history and his hand was "stretched out over *all* nations."

These were difficult days for Judah. Dozens of her fortified cities were laid waste, and as a climax Sennacherib besieged Jerusalem, shutting up Hezekiah "like a caged bird." Hezekiah was so frightened that he sent a message to the king of Assyria's headquarters begging Assyria's withdrawal and promising, "Whatever you impose on me I will bear." The tribute imposed was harsh indeed: "Judah was forced to turn over to Sennacherib three hundred talents of silver, thirty talents of gold, and costly palace and temple treasures, as well as the king's daughters, his harem, and his male and female musicians."[2]

Even so, it is difficult to understand why Sennacherib withdrew without destroying Jerusalem. A plague afflicting the Assyrian forces has been suggested (2 Kings 19:35). Perhaps domestic difficulties made necessary his return. Or possibly rumors of a new Babylonian revolt urgently required the presence of his forces.

In any event, Isaiah had reassured Hezekiah concerning the Assyrian king: "By the way that he came, by the same shall he return, and he shall not come into this city, says the LORD." (Isa. 37:34) His faith and counsel were justified, for Sennacherib never did capture Jerusalem, and the city was spared for another century.

Isaiah was greatly disappointed that the people did not attribute their unexpected deliverance to the hand of God. For the people of Jerusalem did not gather in the temple for thanksgiving but upon the housetops, shouting, singing, and dancing, giving expression to their relief in wild revelry. All they seemed to care about was their own safety.

Isaiah did not claim to know what would eventually happen to the people of Judah. But he firmly believed that God, at the helm of history, would make provision through a faithful remnant for that day of peace he envisioned—when warriors would "beat their swords into plowshares, and their spears into pruning hooks" and not "learn war any more."

ISAIAH'S MESSAGE FOR THE MODERN ERA

The eighth-century prophet of Jerusalem spoke about matters of great consequence in a specific historical situation. He was not prophesying for our benefit in the twentieth century. Yet, because mankind is beset with many of the same problems, and bedevils itself as a result of the same human frailties, much of what Isaiah said still arrests our attention. The names of the nations, the political leaders, and the specific situations have all changed outwardly, but the words of the prophet continue to speak the truth.

What are the major ideas found in chapters 1 to 39 which need to be reiterated today?

The prophet had complete confidence in the judgment and victory of the Lord of history. God was the Ruler of the universe and no one could overrule him. This is a lesson we need to learn: one can ignore God but not escape from him. He is sovereign Power in the world and he has unlimited tenure of office. His existence does not depend upon our vote of confidence.

Today we may be less inclined to think of God as intervening at every point in history as Isaiah did. God may not use wicked nations as his holy instruments, but his judgment allows all nations to reap what they have sown. His long-suffering mercy still blesses us, and his ultimate victory is yet assured.

Isaiah incorporated ethical content into his concept of the holiness of God. God's holiness was not to be found in his unapproachability, in his "wholly otherness," but in his absolute righteousness. As his character is grounded in righteousness, so he demands justice, purity, and nobility of spirit from the children of men.

Today it is not enough to think of God primarily as a comforting presence. Such a God would not, for Isaiah, embody the full meaning of holiness. Rather the ethical demands of the Holy One of Israel should make us uncomfortable as well. As someone has said, the true gospel is one which "comforts the disturbed and disturbs the comfortable." One for whom the presence of God means being coddled by an indulgent Father is not likely to possess a humble and contrite heart. Only the moral exaction of ". . . be perfect, as your heavenly Father is perfect" can prevent smugness and evoke penitence.

Isaiah was wary of basing security policy primarily in alliances and military might. There is some danger, of course, for the United States to be involved in alliances. Such alliances always involve commitment. The U.S. is certainly the centerpiece of the NATO alliance. We are committed to defending

Western Europe against any Soviet attack. Yet we are well aware that U.S. and NATO forces in Europe are little more than a "trip-wire" when posed against the overwhelming forces the Russians and Warsaw Pact nations could employ if they wanted to overrun Western Europe. A U.S. expeditionary force probably could not arrive in time to provide any adequate defense. In reality our strategic nuclear forces furnish the actual deterrent against Russian attack. Our armed forces in Western Europe are largely a symbolic presence. But that symbolic presence involves us in a commitment that is quite costly. The expense of keeping 300,000 troops there runs about $55 billion annually. (This includes salaries, housing, weapons, support forces, etc.)[3] Our commitment to NATO is such that, despite West Germany's relative prosperity over the last ten years, the United States has borne the major cost of forces stationed in that country.

Because of the possible changing nature of component nations in an alliance, such relationships are often tenuous at best. For example, Italy is a participant in NATO, but almost every national election in Italy bears the risk that the Italians will vote the Communists into power. If that happens some day, what would that do to NATO? What would it mean for American-manned nuclear bases placed in Italy?

About 40,000 American troops have been stationed in South Korea. The Carter Administration has committed itself to gradually removing these troops. Throughout the years, however, the bilateral agreement we have had to protect South Korea, in the eyes of the world, has tended to appear that we support that nation's internal policies. Yet during the 70s South Korea, headed by dictator Park Chung Hee, has grossly violated human rights and placed a large number of its political opponents, students and religious leaders in prison for public criticism of the regime. What has such an alliance done for America's image?

Also one wonders how much the ever-increasing stockpile of atomic weapons adds to our security. True, they do add to our overkill capacity. But now that we have such redundant strength that we can destroy the major population and industrial centers of the Soviet Union many times over, how much is enough?[4]

It would seem that only as we enhance the security of the whole world will the United States be truly secure. This means that we can no longer concentrate on policies which *appear* to safeguard our own vital interests yet ignore the security interests of other nations.

Each person must accept personal responsibility for the plight of society. Our contemporary nuclear dilemma is compounded by the feeling of helplessness which weighs upon us once we realize the frightening power of nuclear weapons. As the late President Kennedy stated at American University on June 10, 1963: "A single nuclear weapon contains almost ten times the explosive force delivered by all the Allied air forces in the Second World War." In the face of this magnitude of power we may be tempted to believe that individual action is as futile as shaking one's fist at a hurricane.

But Isaiah engaged in his one-man mission even when confronted with the imminent grim prospect of annihilation. Surely the assumption of personal responsibility today by disciplined individuals could meet with no greater discouragement than he faced.

Late in the summer of 1961, when a bill to create an Arms Control and Disarmament Agency was pending before Congress, few thought the measure had a chance to pass before adjournment. But many responsible Americans poured letters, telegrams, and phone calls into Washington. As a result, in the closing days of Congress the bill passed 5 to 1 in both the Senate and the House. Thus today we have an agency within the government making the necessary studies, hammering out the policies, and contracting for the research which are absolute prerequisites to a safeguarded disarmament treaty.

Deliverance from catastrophe should be used creatively. When the Assyrian siege was lifted, Isaiah deplored the light-footed gaiety and light-headed escapism of the populace. It seemed to him a time for thanksgiving, penitence, and seeking for new directions which would extricate Judah from back-to-back crises.

One cannot compare the relationship of tiny Judah vis-à-vis mighty Assyria with that of the United States vis-à-vis the Soviet Union except perhaps in one aspect: the creative use of a crisis aftermath. Surely in the resolution of the Cuban crisis a reprieve was granted humanity. The God of history delivered both pagan and believer from utter destruction. How is the reprieve being used? If it means only returning to "business as usual" or escaping to frivolities that erase from our minds all serious concerns, then the "nuclear sword of Damocles" has already begun its descent. On the other hand, if more persons are moved to act as though their only real shelter is peace, giving their dedicated attention to the agonizing problems before us, then there is hope indeed.

Selections from First Isaiah

THE FALL OF THE FAITHFUL 1:21–23

How the faithful city
  has become a harlot,
  she that was full of justice!
Righteousness lodged in her,
  but now murderers.
Your silver has become dross,
  your wine mixed with water.
Your princes are rebels
  and companions of thieves.
Every one loves a bribe
  and runs after gifts.
They do not defend the fatherless,
  and the widow's cause does not come to them.

A COMING ERA OF PEACE 2:2–4

It shall come to pass in the latter days
  that the mountain of the house of the LORD
shall be established as the highest of the mountains,
  and shall be raised above the hills;
and all the nations shall flow to it,
  and many peoples shall come, and say:
"Come, let us go up to the mountain of the LORD,
  to the house of the God of Jacob;
that he may teach us his ways
  and that we may walk in his paths."
For out of Zion shall go forth the law,
  and the word of the LORD from Jerusalem.
He shall judge between the nations,
  and shall decide for many peoples;
and they shall beat their swords into plowshares,
  and their spears into pruning hooks;
nation shall not lift up sword against nation,
  neither shall they learn war any more.

THE PROUD BROUGHT LOW 2:12–15, 17–19

For the LORD of hosts has a day
    against all that is proud and lofty,
    against all that is lifted up and high;
against all the cedars of Lebanon,
    lofty and lifted up;
    and against all the oaks of Bashan;
against all the high mountains,
    and against all the lofty hills;
against every high tower,
    and against every fortified wall . . .
And the haughtiness of man shall be humbled,
    and the pride of men shall be brought low;
    and the LORD alone will be exalted in that day.
And the idols shall utterly pass away.
And men shall enter the caves of the rocks
    and the holes of the ground,
from before the terror of the LORD,
    and from the glory of his majesty,
    when he rises to terrify the earth.

THE HAUGHTY DAUGHTERS OF ZION 3:16–17, 24

The LORD said:
Because the daughters of Zion are haughty
    and walk with outstretched necks,
    glancing wantonly with their eyes,
mincing along as they go,
    tinkling with their feet;
the LORD will smite with a scab
    the heads of the daughters of Zion,
    and the LORD will lay bare their secret parts.
Instead of perfume there will be rottenness;
    and instead of a girdle, a rope;
and instead of well-set hair, baldness;
    and instead of a rich robe, a girding of sackcloth;
    instead of beauty, shame.

THE ACQUISITIVE LANDLORDS 5:8–9

Woe to those who join house to house,
    who add field to field,
until there is no more room,

and you are made to dwell alone
in the midst of the land.
The LORD of hosts has sworn in my hearing:
"Surely many houses shall be desolate,
large and beautiful houses, without inhabitant."

HEROES AT DRINKING 5:11, 20–23

Woe to those who rise early in the morning,
that they may run after strong drink,
who tarry late into the evening
till wine inflames them! . . .
Woe to those who call evil good
and good evil,
who put darkness for light
and light for darkness,
who put bitter for sweet
and sweet for bitter!
Woe to those who are wise in their own eyes,
and shrewd in their own sight!
Woe to those who are heroes at drinking wine,
and valiant men in mixing strong drink,
who acquit the guilty for a bribe,
and deprive the innocent of his right!

ISAIAH'S VISION 6:1–8

In the year that King Uzziah died I saw the Lord sitting upon a throne, high and lifted up; and his train filled the temple. Above him stood the seraphim; each had six wings: with two he covered his face, and with two he covered his feet, and with two he flew. And one called to another and said:

"Holy, holy, holy is the LORD of hosts;
the whole earth is full of his glory."

And the foundations of the thresholds shook at the voice of him who called, and the house was filled with smoke. And I said: "Woe is me! For I am lost; for I am a man of unclean lips, and I dwell in the midst of a people of unclean lips; for my eyes have seen the King, the LORD of hosts!"

Then flew one of the seraphim to me, having in his hand a burning coal which he had taken with tongs from the altar. And he touched my mouth, and said: "Behold, this has touched your lips; your guilt is taken away, and your sin forgiven." And I heard the voice of the Lord saying, "Whom shall I send, and who will go for us?" Then I said, "Here am I! Send me."

THE ROD OF GOD'S ANGER 10:5–6

Ah, Assyria, the rod of my anger,
  the staff of my fury!
Against a godless nation I send him,
  and against the people of my wrath I command him,
  to take spoil and seize plunder,
  and to tread them down like the mire of the streets.

THE ILL FATE OF LEGALISM 28:13

Therefore the word of the LORD will be to them
  precept upon precept, precept upon precept,
  line upon line, line upon line,
  here a little, there a little
that they may go, and fall backward,
  and be broken, and snared, and taken.

DEPENDENCE UPON A GRACIOUS GOD 30:12–15, 18

Therefore thus says the Holy One of Israel,
  "Because you despise this word,
  and trust in oppression and perverseness,
  and rely on them;
therefore this iniquity shall be to you
  like a break in a high wall, bulging out, and about to collapse,
  whose crash comes suddenly, in an instant;
and its breaking is like that of a potter's vessel
  which is smashed so ruthlessly
that among its fragments not a sherd is found
  with which to take fire from the hearth,
  or to dip up water out of the cistern."
For thus said the Lord GOD, the Holy One of Israel,
  "In returning and rest you shall be saved;
  in quietness and in trust shall be your strength." . . .
Therefore the LORD waits to be gracious to you;
  therefore he exalts himself to show mercy to you.
For the LORD is a God of justice;
  blessed are all those who wait for him.

THOSE WHO TRUST IN CHARIOTS 31:1, 3

Woe to those who go down to Egypt for help
  and rely on horses,
who trust in chariots because they are many

and in horsemen because they are very strong,
but do not look to the Holy One of Israel
 or consult the Lord! . . .
The Egyptians are men, and not God;
 and their horses are flesh, and not spirit.
When the Lord stretches out his hand,
 the helper will stumble, and he who is helped will fall,
 and they will all perish together.

First Isaiah—A Wise Statesman for Our Modern Era

THE "FAITHFUL" CITY (1:21)

The faithful city has become a harlot.
Senators sanction insobriety
  in the shadow of your Capitol dome.
You take the bloom off the cherry blossom festival by turning
  a joyous celebration into a common brawl.
At the opening of Congress each day,
  the chaplain's fervent prayers on your behalf
  bounce off the newspapers in which you bury your faces.
Cash is delivered to your offices in unmarked envelopes
  as anonymous campaign gifts
  to encourage South Korean subsidies.
Unanimity prevails in voting billions for defense,
  but debate drones on over a few millions for peace research.
Your beloved capital city wins a prize for juvenile delinquency,
  claims the championship for alcohol consumption,
  tolerates dehumanizing slums
  a stone's throw from the nation's capitol.
Your schools rank among the lowest in the nation
  in teaching reading skills.
Yet Congress jealously guards its prerogatives,
  refusing full Home Rule for the District.

SWORDS INTO PLOWSHARES (2:2, 4)

And *it shall come to pass in the latter days*
  men shall catch a vision of God exalted,
  and many peoples shall gather together in a high place.
He shall judge between the nations
  and his judgments shall be their law;
and they shall beat their swords into plowshares,
  their spears into pruning hooks,
their H-bombs into useful sources of energy,
  for the good of all of God's children.

PRIDE BROUGHT LOW (2:12, 17–19)

O people of God, come, let us walk out of the shadows,
   and into the Light shining from heaven.
For the Lord of hosts has a day
   against all that is proud and lofty,
   against all that is lifted up and high,
   against all Empire State buildings,
   against every powerful space craft,
   against all bomb tests everywhere,
   against every Berlin wall,
   against all arrogant transnational corporations,
   against all rattling of rockets and brandishing of missiles,
   against all stockpiling of stocks and bonds.
And the haughtiness of man shall be humbled,
   and the pride of men shall be brought low;
   and the Lord alone will be exalted in that day.
All *idols shall utterly pass away.*
For on that day *men shall enter the caves of the rocks.*
They shall go down into the tombs they think are shelters,
   fleeing from the terror they have created themselves.
In that day the stocks which they have preserved
   will be investments in burning ashes;
their proud sleek Babels will tilt
   like the leaning tower of Pisa;
their walls to keep men in
   will be easily trespassed by rats in the ruins.
The Scriptures will be fulfilled among them:
   they that take up the missile shall go down by the missile.
For men will flee, from the love of God they are to express,
   to inflict terror on their fellows.

AN ORACLE CONCERNING CHRISTIAN CITIZENSHIP
(Isaiah 28:23; 3:14, 15, 6; 8:11, 12; 9:2)

Give ear, and hear my voice;
   hearken and hear my speech,
you who would be responsible Christians:
are you content to ignore the political scene?
pleased to be governed by those worse than yourselves?
Can you pridefully exercise only that freedom
   the ordinary Russian is permitted to have?
Are you fundamentally fearful

about separation of church and state:
    afraid of government dominated by Calvinistic legalism?
Or do you use such arguments falsely,
    as a thin veil for preserving the status quo?
Is politics for you some fifth estate,
    composed of an "untouchable" class?
Are you afraid of getting your hands dirty,
    of making the compromises called for in a pluralistic society?
Do you insist on working only for the impossible perfect?
    And meanwhile the "possible bad" triumphs!
I am weary with your puritanism!
    You were born two hundred years too late!
I remain unimpressed by your political virginity.
    Have you kept your innocence or lost your credibility?
If you are silent, who will condemn the corrupt, saying:
    "the spoil of the poor is in your houses.
    What do you mean by crushing my people,
    by grinding the face of the poor?"
"I would rather work on issues," you say,
    "and stay untainted by the election process."
"It would be better not to get involved
    with the crooks in City Hall."
You may taunt the "death of God" theologians,
    yet you yourself would put me in a box, yea, a "coffin."
Is the smoke of cities burning perfume to your nostrils?
Are the yellow clouds which enshroud urban skylines
    a delight that makes you gasp?
Is the police siren's wail music to your ears?
Are rat-infested slums a sightseeing thrill?
Then my church is discreetly separated from the state,
    and public conscience is safely insulated from government,
    and Christianity is prudently piled on the town's dump.
For then, rejoicing, you may hail your public official:
    "You shall be our leader
    and this heap of ruins
    shall be under your rule."
But it need not come to pass.
Some may judge the Christian who refuses to confine his faith
    to a series of "Thou shalt nots,"
and others will view attempts
    to relate the gospel to government
a subversive activity, a Communist contrivance.

[But] *the Lord spoke thus to me . . . .*
"Do not call conspiracy all that this people call conspiracy,
    and do not fear what they fear,"
[For] *the people who walked in darkness*
    have seen a great light:
They can quote *Robert's Rules*
    as readily as Holy Writ.
They sink their energies in the precinct
    and join the fifteen per cent who vote in local elections,
    knowing lesser officials become governors and senators.
They sacrifice the luxury
    of remaining independent voters.
By redemptive programs, they proclaim:
    "This civilization is not for burning!"
Mature enough to absorb a neighbor's anger,
    yet with a childlike faith in the democratic process,
they strike out, take a public position,
    knowing men will revile them and persecute them,
    and speak all manner of evil against them falsely for my sake.
Willing to enter smoke-filled rooms
    to effectively fight air pollution,
willing to enter their names in an already-won primary,
    to surface issues suppressed by the entrenched victorious,
admitting the guilt of association with a Christ
    who soiled his hands on money-changers.
Oh, non-evaders of the basic!
Be about your Father's business!
Press every doorbell,
    ring every phone,
cast every ballot,
    watch every poll!
Immerse yourselves in hot water,
    —and be clean!

THIS GENERATION'S DAUGHTERS (3:16–26)

O daughters of this generation, preoccupied with vanity,
    doing the hustle as you mince along,
    with platform shoes that raise you up
    but make you risk a fall,
wearing sunglasses, not to shade the eyes,
    but to conceal wanton sidelong glances,
eyes painted wide, but not wide enough

to discern the signs of the times.
Will you lengthen your skirts; or carry a baton to twirl?
You who mouth sweet words of freedom,
    but allow Paris and New York to dictate conformity,
because of your haughtiness and foolishness,
the Lord has sworn:
    that day will come when,
    instead of perfume, there will be the odor of decay,
    instead of high heels, dirty bare feet,
    instead of a girdle, a rope,
    instead of well-tinted hair, snarled dishwater-blonde,
    instead of a dress of signboard scarlet, torn denim.
Awake! that that day may be held back.
Complete your emancipation:
Become human—let the china doll walk off the shelf;
    dress modestly—carry surprises to your marriage bed;
    overcome your obsession with appearance—
        pass by a mirror without looking in.
Let others know who *you* are, unbarricaded by beauty parlor hours.
Cultivate interest in the vital issues of the day,
    not those which lead so quickly to sophisticated boredom.

POSSESSORS POSSESSED (5:8)

Woe unto those who, with unending avarice, add property to property,
    until they are possessed by what they own.
The LORD of hosts has sworn in my hearing:
they shall count houses at midnight instead of sheep.
"Which roof leaks?" "Will he pay the rent?"
    "Shall I put the back forty in the land bank?"
"Are the expenses for the new tenant justified?"
    "Can I unload the land I got stung on?"
"Will they reroute the highway my motel fronts on?"
    "Will blacks move into my subdivision?"

THE DRINKING HEROES (5:22)

Why are you *heroes at drinking* beer? *valiant men in mixing* martinis?
You know that liquor adversely affects the mind,
    that remarkable faculty which elevates you above the animal.
Party-givers, must you loosen up the crowd with a cocktail?
Gracious hosts, would you say frankly to your guests:
    "You are a stupid bore in your natural state.
    Here, have a few drinks to overcome your unbearable dullness,

to stir up the dormant brilliance of your personality!"
Do you advise moderation in using a substance whose first effect weakens
    the power to stop?
Consult your seven million alcoholics.
   Did not each plan to be a moderate drinker?
Will my voice go unheeded, drowned out by raucous drunken laughter?
Then know the consequences of your folly!
Build your mammoth hospitals for alcoholic priests.
Crowd your mental institutions with the chronic whiskey-sodden.
Let blood run down the hills of your highways,
   blood, your beverage mixer for martinis.
Let stewardesses be glorified
   for pushing drinks on airliners.
Let your juveniles get beered up
   for a delinquent spree.
Let your teen-age girls bear illegitimate children
   whose nameless father is gin.
Let your criminals commit unthinkable crimes,
   not contemplated in sober moments.
Pour the rich talent of your writers
   down the sewer with their vomit.

HOW TO AVOID THE GOSPEL

Your prophets must write fiction;
   truth outright is too painful to your hearts.
You place the word "THINK"
   above your IBM machines.
But on your pulpits have you engraved "ENTERTAIN"?
Is there something sacrilegious
   about loving the Lord your God with all your mind?
Your theologians stress eschatology
   and strip bare the ethics of Christ.
They are like shrewd taxpayers looking for loopholes.

THE CALL OF A MAN (6:1–8)

In the year the Space Age was born,
I had a vision of God,
   not through a glass darkly, but face to face.
I sat in church that morning,
   the morning his presence filled the sanctuary.
So overpowering was the experience,
   I was oblivious to others in the congregation.

The all-embracing presence of God
 was closer than the people in my pew.
His thereness was unmistakable.
We had sung a joyful hymn of praise,
 the choir's anthem had lifted my soul out of my body;
 the minister was reading from the Word which suddenly became flesh.
A great Force swept through the sanctuary.
It was as though in that instant of eternity, past and future merged;
 and I knew these people, God's people, intimately;
 and all shared in the divine secret and blessing.
We knew his holiness and he overlooked our frailty.
It was then we were aware that the Lord our God was calling us
 to some majestic task—
as he called Moses in a burning bush,
 the prophets from tending their sheep,
 Jesus from a carpenter's bench,
 and Saul on a Damascus road.
"I'm not good enough," I mumbled, and slumped in my seat.
Perhaps the pastor could represent us,
 or the lay leader, George Johnson.
 Let George do it.
But the Spirit could not be shaken.
For a Voice spoke forth, more ultimatum than request:
 "Whom shall I send, and who will go for us?"
There was no escaping, for the Voice boomed out
 from all four walls, directly at me.
Every face, now so apparent, was turned in my direction.
In tones so steady I barely claimed them for my own,
 my voice replied, *"Here am I! Send me."*

SLEEPING SPIRITS, AWAKE! (10:5–6)

Ah, Russia, *the rod of my anger!*
Ah, Soviets, *the staff of my fury!*
Against a godless nation I send you,
 and against the people of my disappointment I command you.
Though you are wicked and atheistic yourselves,
 I tolerate your power as judgment
to frustrate those who confess me with their lips,
 but ignore me in their daily pursuits.
For you are my spur to stab the flesh,
 that sleeping spirits may awaken from dreams—
dreams that they can utterly deny me,

and walk in the pleasure of their hearts,
that science will prosper them,
that shelters will protect them,
that dollars will save them,
that cosmetics will keep them young,
and the government will keep them when they are old,
that they can put God in a safe-deposit box
    at the corner of Main and Elm.
Now will they examine the truth?
  Look to the faith that is in them?
  Discover the Power that could permeate them?
  Respond to the Love that would again make them human,
    raise them from animal passions,
    and lower them from their pedestal of self-worship?

WHAT GOD REQUIRES

Thus says the Lord:
I delight not in your cash-laden collection plates.
Your pretentious churches are an abomination;
  they vary monotonously from Gothic provincial to factory modern.
On Christmas your gifts are more important
  than the Gift of God.
On Easter you parade your finery before the Deity.
I do not look upon what is on your head,
  but what is in your heart.
Your Sabbaths are not holy days but holidays.
  They exhaust the body and corrupt the soul.
  Bleary-eyed and footsore you turn to Monday.
Do not appear before me with a guilt offering as your price of admission,
or with fashionable attire to entitle you to the best places
  in air-conditioned pews comfortable enough to sleep in.
Air-condition your musty souls; purify your spirits; humble your prideful
    hearts.
Enter your sanctuary prepared to hear the Word of the Lord.
Sing the great hymns without hypocrisy.
When the minister lifts supplication on your behalf,
  read not the bulletin,
  nor count the holes in the accoustical tile.
When the Word is proclaimed for the edification of your soul,
  let not mother prepare next week's menus,
  or father peruse his "accounts due,"
  or sister choose her dress for the prom,

or brother replay Saturday's game.
Let the mind wander only where the conscience leads and the Spirit
    moves,
    watering the desert places of the soul.
Go forth determined to do good:
    to understand the misunderstood,
    to overlook the mistakes of the mistaken,
    to love the unloved,
    to forgive the unforgiven.
Let your heart be immersed in the love of God,
    buoyed up like a swimmer in the salty sea.

INEFFECTIVENESS OF CONTAINMENT

Let the Russian bear, in hibernation for centuries,
    come out of his cave hungry for prowl.
Let the hunter find out he can't slay him,
    or place him in a cage at the zoo,
though armed with tactical atomic weapons,
    and the nets of radar equipment.
He shall leap over the pits of containment,
    and seek berries and honey afar.

THE NEW AMERICAN ISOLATIONISM

Draw near, O America, to hear.
In the thirties you proudly set yourself apart
    from involvement with the world;
but in the sixties you were thoroughly committed
    from Bangkok to Istanbul to Caracas.
Yet today you would isolate others
    as you once insulated yourself:
by placing an embargo on Cuba
    and penalizing unco-operative nations;
by discouraging trade with Vietnam
    and preventing her UN admission.
Long ago you fenced in the Soviet Union
    through non-acceptance in incipient years.
Yet in time you were forced to admit
    her existence as a major power.
On your Archives building you have carved:
    "What is past is prologue."
Thus, can the New Isolationism succeed
    when the Old so clearly demonstrated its failure?

Will you end your days alone
  with a brimming cup of bitterness
  and no companion nation with which to drink?

THE WOLF WITH THE LAMB (11:96)

Hasten that day when none shall *hurt or destroy*
  in all my holy mountain,
and *the earth shall be full of the knowledge of the Lord*
  as the waters cover the sea,
when the beasts of the field and the birds of the air
  shall know their freedom,
  and all shall dwell in a land of peace.
The wolf shall dwell with the lamb, and the leopard shall lie down with the kid,
  and the bear cubs shall not disturb the eagle's nest.

A TALE OF TWO CITIES (13—19)

East Berliners! Do you not know
  that man was born with wings in his heart?
That no wall can contain him,
  no barbed wire catch him in its web?
What he cannot jump over
  he will ram through.
What he cannot swim across
  he will tunnel under.
You have named your country "Democratic,"
  yet your people fear the secret police
  and speak in curfew tones on street corners.
Though your Karl Marx Allee is impressive,
  it bears as little traffic as a back alley.
A new city cries to be erected
  on rubble in which no half-brick fits another.
The Zone regime jams radio
while in the West there rises
  an international center of culture, education, and truth.
The Wall proclaims to other peoples: "Keep out!"
The Free City says to foreign artists and writers: "Come in!"
West Berlin is a shelf
  in a showcase requiring two shelves with no war trophies.
Bark seeks to cover the scar left by a severed limb;
  how long can hate divide what all nature would unite and heal?

THE FREE WORLD (21—23)

The oracle concerning the free world:
O weep, Patrick Henry; shed tears, Thomas Jefferson;
    groan in the grave, Tom Paine!
For the principles you held dear have been perverted.
    Your beloved country does not know her mother.
She has the brow of a harlot, unfaithful to her heritage.
    She would consort with all who are enemies of her enemy,
    though they be not friends of the precepts
        her tradition has upheld.
O America, favorite daughter of my bosom,
    you speak of looking toward a concert of free nations.
But what do you mean by "free"?
    Brazil, oppressor of political prisoners,
        where, with your sanction,
        military rule deposed a democratic regime?
    Iran, where students are harassed, and you do not complain
        so long as oil keeps flowing to the U.S.?
    Chile, whose strong-arm dictatorship came to power
        after you economically strangled its freely-elected government?
    Taiwan, where your generous assistance has
        kept ten million Formosans under the hated heel of Chinese
        nationalists?
    Korea, where a costly war fought for freedom
        has left our beneficiaries the dubious privilege of life
        under an authoritarian military leader?
For this, the freedom you claim to possess
    shall be eaten away by fanatics,
who, in the name of anti-Communism,
    would banish liberty from the land,
    and nonconformity from the nation.
Stay your anger, O Lord!
For my people are like an adolescent prince ascended to the throne.
Spare them, O God, till they reach the wisdom of maturity.

SEPARATION—WHITE FROM BLACK

The oracle concerning race:
why do you make so much of your separation, white from black?
I have never told you I would separate you,
    except as sheep from goats.
How can you expect, America, to get along

with the two-thirds of the world that is colored
   if you can't get along among yourselves?
Your churches reject blacks who seek membership,
   while voicing creeds about the Fatherhood of God.
And many patriotic Americans believe in the freedom of the blacks
   to live next door to somebody else.
Your community leaders cry out for neighborhood schools
   at the same time they keep black families
   from becoming their neighbors.
White parents don't want black children
   bused to superior schools,
or their own children transported to black schools
   they previously ignored.
Why do you make so much of your separation, white from black?
White women go to the beauty parlor to get their hair curled,
   and black women go to get their hair straightened.
White women carefully apply their suntan lotion
   and black women apply their bleaching creams.
A white man is saved from death by black blood of his same type.
For I made of one blood all the nations of the earth,
   and every Christian is called to be color-blind.

COMMUNISM

The oracle concerning Communism:
O nation of the hammer and sickle!
Would you use the hammer
   to pound propaganda into the minds of your people?
And the sickle to cut down all
   who will not conform to the current Kremlin line?
When your five-year plan fails,
   you convert it to a seven-year plan;
when that falters,
   you shift to a twenty-year plan.
When will your people be aware,
   and respond not to Stalin's stick,
   or Khrushchev's elusive carrot?
O virgin lands of Siberia!
When will the sower overtake the reaper
   since the reaper cannot keep up with the sower?
You boast of Communist production,
   yet half your livestock is raised on private plots.
You are proud of your mechanization,

yet within the grounds of your Economic Exhibition,
in front of your Heavy Industry Hall,
two weary men cut the grass with long-handled scythes.
Your industry produces the marvel of a sputnik,
but not the simplest object—a good ball-point pen.
You are a nation where Tolstoy's genius
is recognized only in small print,
and Solzhenitsyn is out of print!
I perceive that you have a sense of humor,
for your censored newspaper is called *Pravda*,
meaning "truth."
You claim to be a classless society, yet your scientists
receive ten times your street-sweepers' wages.
Because all your new apartment buildings look the same,
it would not pay to come home drunk at night,
yet many Muscovites manage this accomplishment,
requiring forty sobering-up stations in your capital city alone.
Your five-room log houses, topped with three TV aerials,
tell an unpublicized story of crowded housing conditions.
Your people's clothing is often rumpled
from storage under beds of closetless apartments.
Your women work on mixing cement and repairing railroad tracks,
on laying brick and tarring roads,
which proves their emancipation from the inequality of the sexes.
You claim to be great advocates of peace,
but dress your schoolboys in military garb.
You offer to support all wars of national liberation,
then crush a genuine revolt in nearby Hungary.
You purport to uphold the virtues of materialism,
yet fear to use your richest natural resource—the free human spirit.
For this, your agriculture shall languish,
and your people shall eat steel;
until the portentous day arrives
when youth educated in science start to think about politics;
when they begin to know what the outside world knows,
penetrating an Iron Curtain that can keep people in,
but not ideas out.

"THE SPIRIT GIVETH LIFE" (28:13)

Oracle to the ministers:
Therefore the word of the Lord will be to them
line upon line, table upon table, figures upon figures.

You preachers know all the statistics, from pastors' salaries
  to memberships of churches.
Must you all get the bishop's eye?
Does your ministry have to be judged by comparative annual reports?
Must you pile member on member, budget on budget,
  building on building, to be "successful"?
Would not other vital statistics reveal the real strength of a church?
  How many members walked out on sermons last year?
  How many pounds of clothing were contributed to overseas relief?
  How much canned food was collected for the anti-hunger program?
  How many marriages were kept from going on the rocks?
  How many high-quality youth are candidates for the ministry?
  How many missionaries are supported through special gifts?

BARREN PLANS AND ALLIANCES (30:1–2)

"Woe to the rebellious children," says the Lord,
  "who carry out a plan, but not mine;
  and who make a league, but not of my spirit,"
  who invade Cuba without seeking my counsel,
  who engage in illegal overflights without asking my advice.
They have their plans:
  how to become rich on real estate working weekends;
  how to retire and loaf before 30;
  how to have a tranquil soul and not give a hang
    if the world goes to hell.
They have their alliances:
  a SEATO that guaranteed any Asian war
    would be a "white foreign intrusion,"
  a NATO dominated by Germans
    not known for restraint in launching war.
Their plans are not the Divine Plan.
In their alliances I cannot be their Ally.

THE CIRCLE OF DEATH (30:12, 13)

Thus says the Lord:
"Because you despise this word,
  and trust in oppression and perverseness,
  and rely on them;
therefore this iniquity shall be to you
  like the smashing of a tool into dozens of pieces,
  so minute that not a piece is found large enough for a hammer,
  or sharp enough for a chisel.

Some speak lightly of your atomic destruction,
   claiming your society could be rebuilt in a few years.
Rebuild your industry with machines!
   We have no machines.
Rebuild your machines with tools!
   We have no tools.
Rebuild your tools with castings!
   We have no castings.
Rebuild your castings with ore!
We have no ore.
Dig your ore!
   We have no machines."

RESPONSE TO GOD'S GRACE (30:15, 18)

For thus said the Lord God,
   "In returning and rest you shall be saved;
   in quietness and in trust shall be your strength."
Therefore the Lord waits to be gracious to you;
   therefore he exalts himself to show mercy to you.
For the Lord is a God of justice;
   blessed are all those who wait for him.
Is thunder heard in an uninhabited desert?
Can sunshine cause an unplanted garden to grow?
Will the most delicious dinner be served
   to invited guests unarrived?
Can the choicest award be presented
   if the recipient declines?
Neither can God give you his richest blessing,
   unless you are willing to unwrap his gifts.
Wait upon the Lord, and renew your faith.

WOE TO THOSE— (31)

Woe to those who exalt sex,
   who enrich themselves by inflaming the passions,
   who publish pornographic literature,
   who transform a beautiful woman into a goddess of love
   and exploit her through magazines, movies, and television.
Therefore your youth grow lax in morals,
   the bonds of marriage are loosened,
   and crimes of lust abound in your cities.
Woe to those who carve upon their marble buildings,
   "Equal justice under law,"

yet allow an Equal Rights Amendment
  to languish in their legislatures.
Woe to those who preach democracy
  yet shut their schools rather than admit black children,
  and burn school buses when they dare protest.
Woe to those who add air base to air base,
  who encircle the globe with their bombers,
  and plant their missiles on reluctant soil.
Yet shall they feel no security,
  for all their farflung armaments.
Woe to those who talk glibly of peace,
  yet they brandish the threat of annihilation.
Therefore they shall live in fear,
  and none shall trust them
  until they learn to trust in my Spirit,

says the Lord of the universe.

FEEDING THE HUNGRY (32:6)

For the fool speaks folly . . .
  to utter error concerning the Lord,
to leave the craving of the hungry unsatisfied,
  and to deprive the thirsty of drink.
O you Christians, dear to my heart,
I will not listen to your shopworn words!
  that the world needs to satisfy its spiritual hunger
that we must share the Scriptures with the infidel
  when some of your beneficiaries are hungry enough
  to eat the bark off trees.
What would you do?
  stuff gilt-edged paper into their mouths?
  tell them "the Lord will take care of you"
when their distended bellies
  belie that comforting falsehood?
No! Start sharing out of your surplus
  and out of your thoughtless consumption.
Begin to feed my sheep so they can get their minds off their bodies
  and the security of their next meal.
Perhaps, then, "spiritual" concerns can penetrate their consciousness
for the Word of God becomes flesh
  when you care about those
  who are all skin and bones.

WOMEN'S RIGHTS (32:9, 11)

Rise up, you women who are at ease, hear my voice;
  you complacent daughters, give ear to my speech.
Tremble, you women who are at ease,
  shudder, you complacent ones.
For too long you have endured discrimination;
  for your rights have been cast under foot,
  your freedom held in check.
For your sex has been confined to home and children,
  and when you ventured out
  your fingers were glued to typewriter keys.
Your sister women were the only ones
  who knew how to change diapers, wash dishes,
  and run the vacuum cleaner.
Your sex did not need to be educated—
  all they had to do was learn to cook and catch a man.
Stop being so complacent!
Those who are demanding rights
  are doing it in the name of *all* women.
Do you want all your options closed
  so you cannot ever dream of being
  a carpenter, a banker, or a sea captain?
Wake up, O ye women!
Claim your rightful destiny,
  and your right to equal pay.
Stop getting your way through guile or subservience or sex persuasion.
  Can you not come into your own on your own?
Can you only become wealthy
  by surviving your spouse?
Is your major route to Congress
  through an early death of husband?
Must your boss meet catastrophe
  for you to rise to responsibility?
Come, now, learn by yourself
  that the squeaky door gets the oil.
Squeak! Speak up! Demand! Lobby!
Woman was created in God's own image
  and God shows no partiality.
For in the sight of the Lord
  they are neither white nor black,
  slave nor free, male nor female,

but all are one in Christ Jesus.
So, be what you were made for,
   assume your rightful role,
   achieve the equality that is your destiny.
From Seneca Falls to the E.R.A.
   help women's rights be our country's way.
Do not let America down.
   Lift your sisters up
   from the pedestal on which they've been placed.
For I have a vision of a different world:
   where a girl can grow up to be the President;
where half the resources of the nation
   are no more cast on the rubbish heap;
where women can swim out of the typing pool
   and into the perilous world;
where maturing females are no longer locked
   into rigid stereotypes,
    "framed" by the false images
   of children's books and TV soap operas;
where women are not "protected"
   from all the important things that happen
   by serving in the ladies' auxiliary.
For I see a more equitable world:
   where women can *go out* to work
   without being accused of child desertion;
or, they may choose to stay at home,
   rear children, and practice the domestic arts;
where women are respected for what they can do,
   and not just for how they look;
where the best positions are open
   to the best persons in the work force;
where no job is beneath a man
   nor above a woman;
where girls can be educated to their full capacity
   and men can work as typists without a smirk or frown;
where a famous surgeon may be a woman
   and the "charming helpmate" of a Senator, a man;
where a man may live on
   his deceased wife's Social Security;
where every wife holds equal property rights
   and every homemaker's contribution
   is recognized for social value;

where all women are fully free and equal human beings
  and may advance according to their own abilities.
Bring forth that day
  when the sun will rise on our sisters
  without setting on our brothers;
when women will "beat their pots and pans
  into printing presses
  and weave their cloth into protest banners,
  nations of women shall lift up their voices
  with nations of other women
      neither shall they accept discrimination any more."*

THE PLEASANT LITTLE WAR

Your military leaders say:
let us never again have a general war;
  for an all-out nuclear war would destroy civilization.
But let us be prepared for limited wars—
  wars in which nuclear weapons would be used on military targets only;
  conventional wars in which only tactical nuclear arms would be brought
      into play;
  wars in outer space where the earth could be spared.
"Let us not give up war," said the general.
  "Let us keep it within bounds,
  a gentlemen's affair."
Thus says the Lord:
how can you establish rules for modern war?
Military drills may have their "war games,"
but once the battle is joined,
  and the days and the months pile bitterness upon hostility,
  then the shock of bombing open cities wears thin;
  the Coventrys become Dresdens and Hamburgs;
  and the Pearl Harbors, Hiroshimas;
  and no open guilt is admitted.
Can you count on a "little nuclear war,"
  or a conflict of military forces only?
Such strategy based on a "friendly exchange"
  taxes the imagination beyond wondering.
Escalation would surely take place.
The vengeance that is mine would be taken by men

*The material in quotes was written as a paraphrase by Mary Chagnon of Duluth, Minnesota
and obtained from the Women's Equity Action League.

into their own hands.
Remember, O man!
The ultimate weapon has been used in every major war.
In World War I,
   poison gas;
in World War II,
   the atomic bomb.

THE DEATH PENALTY (Excerpts from Isaiah 38)

I am consigned to the gates of [Hell]
   for the rest of my years . . .
I shall not see the Lord
   in the land of the living;
I shall look upon man no more
   among the inhabitants of the world . . .
Like a weaver I have rolled up my life;
   he cuts me off from the loom;
from day to night thou dost bring me to an end . . .
My eyes are weary with looking upward . . .
All my sleep has fled
   because of the bitterness of my soul . . .
Oh, restore me to health and make me live!
for thou hast held back my life
   from the pit of destruction,
for thou hast cast all my sins
   behind thy back . . .
The Lord will save me,
   and we will sing to stringed instruments
all the days of our life,
   at the house of the Lord.

I wish it were so
   with all of thy children.
I am among 600 on death row
   and we are waiting, waiting, waiting
   and at the same time
   knowing, knowing, knowing
   that most Americans will our death.
Many of them even want us
   killed on public television.
They want to say to their children,
   "See, that's what

will happen to you
    if you're not good."
Since most Americans no longer
    believe in the devil,
they want to test their fellow citizens out
    and see if they believe
    in the electric chair!
But I know, O God, where my fate rests.
It rests with "nine old men,"
    most of whom have never read the Bible through,
    but they are supposed to be wise.
Most of them don't have much
    life left in this world.
I wonder if they will value it for me?
Yes, I'm guilty, but there
    may be some among the 600 who are not;
if their lives are snuffed
    out by the state,
who will restore them
    when the real criminals confess?
As for me, you can take my life
    if you want to.
But I'm not like Gary Gilmore;
    I don't want to die.
And I would give anything
    to bring the shopkeeper I
    killed back to life.
It was in a moment of
    passion; he fired at me,
    and I fired back.
    He dropped, clutching his chest.
The gun was loaded: curse all guns!
    I wouldn't be here if it weren't for a gun.

You say: a life for a life
But I say I made a mistake
    —a regrettably terrible mistake;
    why compound it?
Is it possible that the State,
    acting on behalf of *all* citizens,
    has the right to take human life?
What about the fifteen percent of Americans

who oppose capital punishment;
can the state act for them,
    nullify *their* consciences?
While the state is serving as an instrument
    for those who demand *justice*,
can it, at the same time,
    ignore those who, out of *conscience*, reject any state-imposed death?
Yes, I do believe the death penalty
    is "cruel and unusual punishment."
Few would deny it is "unusual";
    but is it "cruel"?
Is it cruel to be burned to death?
Or is it painless to sleep away with g
The pain comes in knowing
    that *all* of society is doing this to you;
that the state is acting
    dispassionately for all of its citizens.
It makes my mother throw the switch
    and my son turn on the gas.
It makes my father put the rope around my neck
    and my wife give me the injection.
No one in the whole nation
    can raise a staying hand.
If this is not "cruel,"
    the word has no meaning.
Do you who call yourselves Christian
    think I can't change?
    that my continuing life has no value?
    that I am unworthy of redemption in this world?
    that, in me, the spark of the Divine has been snuffed out?
I beg of you to read the Scriptures once again.
For there I have read in my darkened cell
    about the two most important persons of the Old Testament:
Moses, who murdered an Egyptian
    and fled in the night
but went on to become
    the giver of the Law of Life.
David, who "arranged" the
    death of Bathsheba's husband,
    yet admired in all Christendom
    as the eloquent shepherd-king.
Is there a chance for me?

Or in your New Testament,
Paul, persecutor of Christians,
    held the coats of those stoning Stephen,
    and he was "consenting to his death."
And from being accomplice to the murder of an innocent
    Paul rose to be the major leader and missionary of the early church.
Is there a chance for me?
And so, I implore your mercy
    in the name of Christ
    who forgave enemies,
    asked his friends to put up their swords
    and came unto those in prison.

THE RUSSIAN ORTHODOX CHURCH*

An oracle concerning the Russian Orthodox Church:

It was the week of the October Revolution.
Russian Orthodox leaders were gathered in solemn assembly.
Many ecclesiastical matters graced the agenda,
    while violence stalked the land,
    and blood ran free in the palaces and streets of the nation;
    while a cause was born
    that would shake the foundations of the world.
For days the priests debated; the hierarchy held spirited discussions
    on a most important issue before them,
    plaguing their commission on ritual.
"What color stoles," they queried one another,
    "shall we wear during the seasons of the year?"
Affable priests, silent prophets, and simple peasants
    go down to the pit together.

*It is only fair to say that the Sobor, or church assembly, *did* understand that the Revolution threatened the position of the Russian Orthodox Church. However, rather than being concerned with the problems facing the peasants and workers, problems which spawned the Revolution, the Sobor focused its attention upon the reestablishment of the Patriarchate so that the church might be more effective in dealing with the state as it sought to protect its own interests. The church favored the continuance of the war and opposed peace talks with Germany—this despite the fact that both soldiers and citizenry were sick of the conflict. Recommendations were sent to the Constituent Assembly (never successfully convened) which largely centered around maintenance of ecclesiastical prerogatives, such as: the tax-free status of church property; the continuance of parochial schools; the right of the church to support from state funds.

Control of the Sobor was in the hands of the ultra-conservative upper clergy most of the time although the liberal minority in the assembly fought a vigorous but losing battle during the early months. Thus, it can be said that the mainstream of church leadership was out of touch with a populace desiring more than status quo. (For a thorough discussion of the spirit and action of the Sobor, see *The Russian Church and the Soviet State* by John Shelton Curtiss, Boston: Little, Brown and Company, 1955, pp. 9–70.)

The priests are wearing black,
  and the season is one of mourning.
It is a third of a century later.
Russian church leaders are again in assembly.
They gather together at New Delhi with the World Council of Churches.
They are in the fraternal company of Christians from near and far,
  brothers who have officially received them,
  together with their thirty million members.
Surely the church is the only institution
  leaping over man-made walls and piercing through Iron Curtains
  to embrace, in a fellowship of love, citizens of enemy nations.
The debates again are spirited; divergent views emerge.
Yet on this the Russians agree:
  "Communism is a judgment upon us,
  for rendering the gospel irrelevant!"
Can American churches and constituent Christians
become so involved in petty peripheries,
  in building campaigns and finance drives,
  in spaghetti suppers and routine ritual,
that there is no time to be the church,
  to bless mankind as peacemakers,
  to assume our role as "sons of God,"
  to make the gospel relevant to our day?

THE CONTROL OF POWER

How can you handle your mounting power
  unless you turn to another Power,
  who gives direction as well as force?
Your atomic physicists estimate there are extant in the world
  sixty thousand megatons of nuclear power.
Your population experts estimate there are extant in the world
  three billion inhabitants populating our planet.
Simple arithmetic then reveals
  that in terms of equivalent nuclear power,
There are twenty tons of TNT
  for every man, woman, and child on earth!
In your Fourth of July celebrations,
  you have outlawed dangerous fireworks;
in your state legislatures,
  you have established some controls over rifles and pistols.
Yet consider the international community,
  unable to outlaw nuclear weapons,

weapons not to maim a few adults or kill a few children,
  but which threaten all humanity.
Not only are you unable to eliminate dangerous arms,
  but you face the alarming prospect of the imminent spread of atomic
      weapons.
Who will be next in the Nuclear Club?
  An Israel perpetually feuding with Egypt?
  A Brazil whose power is in the hands of a military regime?
  A South Africa surrounded by enemies on its own continent?
  A Germany which took initiative in two world wars?
Act! Move! Agree! Decide! Turn back from the abyss!

BY WHOSE PRINCIPLES?

Have you not heard the injunction of the Lord?
  "If thine enemy hunger, feed him."
Yet there are those among you who say,
  "Let them starve, and let hunger be the curse of Communism.
  Let us not show mercy and love,
  but be as cold and calculating and ruthless as the enemy.
  Let's win for a change!"
Is your memory so short?
A man in Central Europe said,
  "Let us waste no love on Jews, spare no mercy to captured Poles.
  Blot out the Bible from your mind.
  The sword is more important than the Cross."
That man wanted to win, too.
  His name was Hitler.
No, saith the Lord, do not adopt the attitudes or ape the methods
  of those who hold an alien philosophy.
What does it profit you, if in the struggle with your adversary,
  you become identical with him?
You have your own ideals to promote,
  your own principles to uphold.
It does not take fire to put out fire,
  but water—Living Water.
Is your enemy hungry?
  Feed him.
Does he slander?
  Bless.
Is he hostile?
  Show friendship.
Does he act belligerent?
  Be understanding.

Is his mouth full of lies?
  Speak the truth in love.

THE GIFT OF PEACE

Many gifts have been received by the United Nations
  from the various countries of the world.
Symbolically they adorn the temple of the nations.
There are statues from Greece,
  paintings from Brazil,
  woodcarvings from Indonesia.
But the most impressive symbol enhancing the Parliament of Man
  is an empty space—
the dome of the General Assembly, left incomplete
  to signify the unfinished tasks of peace.
Fly a white dove to the dome!
Crown it with a wreath of olive branches!

IV | JONAH

HIS TIMES AND OURS

The Life And Times Of Jonah
The Major Teaching of Jonah
Jonah's Message for the Modern Era

THE BOOK OF JONAH

Jonah Flees from God's Call
In His Distress Jonah Repents
Nineveh Repents at Jonah's Preaching
The Rebuke of Jonah

PROVINCIAL PROPHET IN A JET AGE

The Vision
The Escape
The Speech
The Aftermath

Jonah—His Times and Ours

In the latter part of the fourth century B.C. the Jewish people were under Greek rule. Having been subject to a succession of foreign conquerors—Assyria, Babylonia, Persia—the Jews had almost forgotten the concept of God's universal love for all nations. They looked forward to the day when God would exalt them and give vent to his wrath upon their neighbors and overlords. Judaism had become ingrown, with an emphasis upon legalism, ritual, and the priestly functions.

During this era an anonymous Jewish religious thinker wrote a parable to jolt his countrymen out of their provincialism, to rekindle the missionary zeal of Second Isaiah, to remind them they were chosen by God to be a light to the Gentiles. He took as the central figure of his tale a prophet named Jonah who typified Jewish nationalism and scorn toward heathen nations.

Jonah is commanded by God to go to Nineveh, an Assyrian city noted for its wickedness, to warn the people to repent. But Jonah cares very little about the redemption of any people other than the Israelites. So instead of heading east to Nineveh he sails west toward Tarshish, a Spanish port as far west as ships from Judah ever ventured.

In resisting the call of God, Jonah is subject to a series of calamities— a terrible storm at sea and his well-known episode with the great fish. In the midst of all this, God's insistent call comes once more to Jonah to go to Nineveh and preach to her people so they may change their ways and be spared destruction. This time Jonah heeds the Lord's request. He travels to Nineveh and preaches in the name of God to its wicked inhabitants. "Yet forty days," cries Jonah, "and Nineveh shall be overthrown!"

Then the unforeseen happens. The Ninevites actually do repent and as a token of their repentance put on sackcloth and ashes. But Jonah does not respond as one would expect a prophet to behave. He is angry and bitter because God has seen fit to show compassion upon these wayward foreigners who have turned from their sin. Far from desiring the salvation of the Ninevites, he had hoped to be an eyewitness to their destruction.

While Jonah sits outside the city waiting to see what action God will

---

*Although the book of Jonah was written in the fourth century B.C. and reflects that era, the author appropriated for his main character a relatively obscure prophet, "Jonah, the son of Amittai," who lived in Israel about 785 B.C. (See 2 Kings 14:25). For this reason Jonah is introduced at this point.

take, a vigorous gourd grows up and provides the prophet with shade. When the next day it withers, Jonah is resentful because God has let the comfort-bringing vine perish. The Lord then asks Jonah why, if he had pity upon a shortlived plant, should not God himself take pity upon a city containing thousands of innocent people.

THE MAJOR TEACHING OF JONAH

No pre-Christian biblical book expresses the concept of God's universal love as clearly as does the parable of Jonah. One might draw an interesting comparison with Jesus' parable of the good Samaritan. In both accounts those who ignore God's will were popularly considered the religious leaders of their day—the provincial prophet in Jonah and the priests and Levites of Jesus' story. On the other hand, the people who did God's will—the repentant Ninevites and the good Samaritan—were despised by devout Jews at the time the stories were told.

JONAH'S MESSAGE FOR THE MODERN ERA

The concept of the universal love of God is one which the author of Jonah could well share with our contemporary world. "National self-interest," which is the guideline of the foreign policies of most countries, often runs counter to the expression of sincere compassion for the well-being of other peoples.

For example, the United States allows approximately $3 billion per year* for its economic aid program to help answer human needs on our planet. At the same time we provide the same amount annually for our program in unpopulated outer space. While any bill with the word "space" in it tends to jet-propel its way intact through both the House and Senate, the foreign aid bill traditionally is discussed by four committees of Congress and often has been slashed in varying degrees by each one.

An experience related by Dr. Darrell Randall typifies our attitudes toward world-wide human needs. Dr. and Mrs. Randall, Christian missionaries to Africa, were once traveling by train from Elizabethville to Johannesburg. Their train passed through a section of Africa which periodically suffered severe drought and famine. During these hunger seasons Africans often had to live on roots until the next crop was harvested. At supper time they pulled into the station of a small town in that destitute area. The two missionaries were in the dining car enjoying a sumptuous meal. As the train stopped, a crowd of Africans, mostly children, gathered about the dining car and peered hungrily through the glass.

---

*estimated appropriation for fiscal 1978

Needless to say, the Randalls could not enjoy their food under these circumstances. At the suggestion of the porter they did what most sensitive persons would do—they reached up and pulled down the curtain.

Looking back, Dr. Randall concluded that this is the way, too often, we American Christians react to the third of the world which is always hungry. These marginal-living people of Africa, Asia, and Latin America are no longer in ignorance about the world situation. They are very much aware of our abundance. In fact, they are peering through our window. And frequently we pull down the shade so as not to be haunted by our disturbed consciences. However, on the other hand, through government assistance such as Food for Peace and through the missionary and world service efforts of our churches, we can make credible our faith that God's love and mercy extends to all.

If we are to give spiritual expression to the universality at the heart of the book of Jonah, we must be concerned about narrowing the gap between the "have" and "have not" nations, but that is not enough. We should also seek to bridge the chasm between East and West. The American Christian should seek every opportunity to express good will toward people in the Soviet Union. One heartening step toward reconciliation was taken when the thirty-million-member Russian Orthodox Church was received into the World Council of Churches in 1961. Thus the church is the only non-governmental institution which embraces in a fellowship of love the citizens of adversary nations.

In March 1963, top leaders of the Russian Orthodox Church were guests of the National Council of Churches in the United States. One day while attending meetings at the Interchurch Center in New York City they were picketed by a right-wing group who felt it was unpatriotic and disloyal to associate with the Russians. In the evening, as the Russian churchmen left a dinner at Riverside Church, they were greeted by more than one hundred students from nearby Union Theological Seminary, who broke into singing "In Christ There Is No East or West."

Edna St. Vincent Millay in her poem "Renascence" wrote:

> The world stands out on either side
> No wider than the heart is wide;
> Above the world is stretched the sky,—
> No higher than the soul is high.[1]

The author of Jonah calls us to widen our hearts and to lift up our souls "to let the face of God shine through."

The Book of Jonah

Now the word of the LORD came to Jonah the son of Amittai, saying, "Arise, go to Nineveh, that great city, and cry against it; for their wickedness has come up before me." But Jonah rose to flee to Tarshish from the presence of the LORD. He went down to Joppa and found a ship going to Tarshish; so he paid the fare, and went on board, to go with them to Tarshish, away from the presence of the LORD.

But the LORD hurled a great wind upon the sea, and there was a mighty tempest on the sea, so that the ship threatened to break up. Then the mariners were afraid, and each cried to his god; and they threw the wares that were in the ship into the sea, to lighten it for them. But Jonah had gone down into the inner part of the ship and had lain down, and was fast asleep. So the captain came and said to him, "What do you mean, you sleeper? Arise, call upon your god! Perhaps the god will give a thought to us, that we do not perish."

And they said to one another, "Come, let us cast lots, that we may know on whose account this evil has come upon us." So they cast lots, and the lot fell upon Jonah. Then they said to him, "Tell us, on whose account this evil has come upon us? What is your occupation? And whence do you come? What is your country? And of what people are you?" And he said to them, "I am a Hebrew; and I fear the LORD, the God of heaven, who made the sea and the dry land." Then the men were exceedingly afraid, and said to him, "What is this that you have done!" For the men knew that he was fleeing from the presence of the LORD, because he had told them

Then they said to him, "What shall we do to you, that the sea may quiet down for us?" For the sea grew more and more tempestuous. He said to them, "Take me up and throw me into the sea; then the sea will quiet down for you; for I know it is because of me that this great tempest has come upon you." Nevertheless the men rowed hard to bring the ship back to land, but they could not, for the sea grew more and more tempestuous against them. Therefore they cried to the LORD, "We beseech thee, O LORD, let us not perish for this man's life, and lay not on us innocent blood; for thou, O LORD, hast done as it pleased thee." So they took up Jonah and threw him into the sea; and the sea ceased from its raging.

Then the men feared the LORD exceedingly, and they offered a sacrifice to the LORD and made vows.

IN HIS DISTRESS JONAH REPENTS

And the LORD appointed a great fish to swallow up Jonah; and Jonah was in the belly of the fish three days and three nights.

Then Jonah prayed to the LORD his God from the belly of the fish, saying,

> "I called to the LORD, out of my distress,
> and he answered me;
> out of the belly of Sheol I cried,
> and thou didst hear my voice.
> For thou didst cast me into the deep,
> into the heart of the seas,
> and the flood was round about me;
> all thy waves and thy billows
> passed over me.
> Then I said, 'I am cast out
> from thy presence;
> how shall I again look
> upon thy holy temple?'
> The waters closed in over me,
> the deep was round about me;
> weeds were wrapped about my head
> at the roots of the mountains.
> I went down to the land
> whose bars closed upon me for ever;
> yet thou didst bring up my life from the Pit,
> O LORD my God.
> When my soul fainted within me,
> I remembered the LORD;
> and my prayer came to thee,
> into thy holy temple.
> Those who pay regard to vain idols
> forsake their true loyalty.
> But I with the voice of thanksgiving
> will sacrifice to thee;
> what I have vowed I will pay.
> Deliverance belongs to the LORD!"

And the LORD spoke to the fish, and it vomited out Jonah upon the dry land.

NINEVEH REPENTS AT JONAH'S PREACHING

Then the word of the LORD came to Jonah the second time, saying, "Arise, go to Nineveh, that great city, and proclaim to it the message that I tell you." So Jonah arose and went to Nineveh, according to the word of the LORD. Now Nineveh was an exceedingly great city, three days' journey in breadth. Jonah began to go into the city, going a day's journey. And he cried, "Yet forty days, and Nineveh shall be overthrown!" And the people of Nineveh believed God; they proclaimed a fast, and put on sackcloth, from the greatest of them to the least of them.

Then tidings reached the king of Nineveh, and he arose from his throne, removed his robe, and covered himself with sackcloth, and sat in ashes. And he made proclamation and published through Nineveh, "By the decree of the king and his nobles: Let neither man nor beast, herd nor flock, taste anything; let them not feed, or drink water, but let man and beast be covered with sackcloth, and let them cry mightily to God; yea, let every one turn from his evil way and from the violence which is in his hands. Who knows, God may yet repent and turn from his fierce anger, so that we perish not?"

When God saw what they did, how they turned from their evil way, God repented of the evil which he had said he would do to them; and he did not do it.

THE REBUKE OF JONAH

But it displeased Jonah exceedingly, and he was angry. And he prayed to the LORD and said, "I pray thee, LORD, is not this what I said when I was yet in my country? That is why I made haste to flee to Tarshish; for I knew that thou art a gracious God and merciful, slow to anger, and abounding in steadfast love, and repentest of evil. Therefore now, O LORD, take my life from me, I beseech thee, for it is better for me to die than to live." And the LORD said, "Do you do well to be angry?" Then Jonah went out of the city and sat to the east of the city, and made a booth for himself there. He sat under it in the shade, till he should see what would become of the city.

And the LORD God appointed a plant, and made it come up over Jonah, that it might be a shade over his head, to save him from his discomfort. So Jonah was exceedingly glad because of the plant. But when dawn came up the next day, God appointed a worm which attacked the plant, so that it withered. When the sun rose, God appointed a sultry east wind, and the sun beat upon the head of Jonah so that he was faint; and he asked that he might die, and said, "It is better for me to die than to live." But God said to Jonah, "Do you do well to be angry for the plant?" And he said, "I do well to be angry, angry enough to die." And the LORD said, "You pity the plant, for which you did not labor, nor did you make it grow, which came into being in a night, and perished in a night. And should not I pity Nineveh, that great city, in which there are more than a hundred and twenty thousand persons who do not know their right hand from their left, and also much cattle?"

Jonah—Provincial Prophet in a Jet Age

His name was Jonah Burke, but his close friends all called him Jon. As a wealthy industrialist, he was the owner of a firm on the West Coast known to be the beneficiary of lucrative defense contracts year after year. Jon Burke was proud of his patriotism, although he had no war record to boast of. During World War II he had been much too busy making huge profits manufacturing airplane parts. During the fifties, when he moved into missile component production the company which bore his name offered profit-anxious investors plenty of "guilt-edged" security.

Yet despite his absorbing business interests, Jon Burke was known as a man of God. He attended worship with the same regularity that he took his vitamins. He was a double-tither in his church and had been a heavy contributor to its extensive building programs.

During the 1960s, in the name of God and country, he felt he had been called to organize a great crusade to save mankind. The slogan for the new movement was "Peace through triumph over Communism." Great throngs gathered in giant rallies under the crusade's banner. This gave Jon Burke an excellent opportunity to practice his outstanding oratorical ability. The core of his message was this: "Atheistic Communism is encroaching on our freedom everywhere in the world. We must expose this menace to a free and competitive society here at home and awaken our fellow Americans to the threat abroad. Above all, we must take the initiative—not just react to pressure but put Communism on the defensive." Though no lists of Burke Society members were ever made public, it was rumored that the movement had hundreds of thousands, perhaps millions, of supporters.

As the movement grew, it was increasingly difficult to keep disreputable characters out, and undoubtedly a number of crackpots joined—this despite the unrelenting criticism by the Burke Society of Communist infiltration in the State Department, the AFL-CIO, the churches, etc.

THE VISION

Arriving home from a rally late one evening, Jon went to bed exhausted and fell into a dreamless sleep. In the middle of the night he felt himself stabbed suddenly awake. The room was dark, but he heard a voice call to him: "Jonah, Jonah!"

"Yes, Lord!" said Jon Burke, breaking out in a cast-iron sweat.

"Listen, you are to be my chosen servant to speak to my beloved children, the Russians."

"Your *be-beloved?*"

"Yes, like all mankind they are my beloved—though erring—children."

"Bu-but why me?"

"They need my message and you are able to give it to them."

"But they do not deserve salvation, and besides, they surely will never listen to me!"

But now the room was empty and silent—except for Jon's heavy breathing and the thumping of his heart. Contemplating the meaning of his experience, Jon Burke did not rest well the balance of the night. A less spiritual man might have ignored such an apparition, but the matter greatly troubled Jon Burke's thoughts.

The next day a strange-looking, well-postmarked piece of mail arrived at the Burke residence. It was from the Soviet Union and inside the letterhead read: MOSCOW PEACE CONGRESS. Jon found that he was invited to speak before that body early next summer. Burke had heard of this type of annual gathering before but had dismissed it as a lightly veiled attempt on the part of the Communists to influence and indoctrinate naive representatives of neutral and Western Nations. The word "peace" in such instances served as enticing bait.

So plagued was Jon's conscience for the next few weeks that he could neither work nor sleep. The last place he wished to go was Moscow. The last thing he wanted to do was to deliver an address at the seat of the Kremlin.

THE ESCAPE

Needing time to think the whole thing over, and perhaps put it out of his mind entirely, Jon decided on a spring vacation—a yachting trip to the Bermudas. He gathered a few business associates together, flew across country, and together they shoved off from Tampa Bay where he had stored one of his boats. He throttled down the coast and through the Keys and headed east.

Storm warnings had been sounded in the vicinity, but the weather was open and clear immediately ahead. At a leisurely thirty knots the *Patriot* eased by Cuba some twenty-five nautical miles to the north. Jon had cautioned his fellow crewmen against brushing too close to the "Devil's Island of the Caribbean" for fear of contamination.

When Cuba was a half-day's view behind, Jon sighted a crippled fishing vessel on the port side ahead. It was a small Russian trawler listing precariously. Apparently its communications equipment was out of order for there was no response to radio signals. But the *Patriot* crew could see the Russian seamen waving wildly upon the deck of the uptilted side. "We just can't let them sink, Russians or no Russians!" muttered Burke. He drew alongside the obviously doomed vessel, risking the peril of being sucked under should the trawler suddenly decide to sleep on the bed of the sea.

There were eight men aboard—all smelling of fish, but the *Patriot* made room for them—at considerable inconvenience to the crew of business-men. Needless to say, piscatorial fragrance predominated over the pleas-ant perfume of lingering after-shave lotion.

Fortunately, one of the Russian fishermen had had some contact with Americans at the close of World War II and knew some simple English. Their ship had been hit by a sudden squall, he revealed. So great had been the impact of the waves that even the lifeboats had been broken up. They had headed toward Cuba but didn't quite make it.

The *Patriot* redirected its course toward Puerto Rico, the closest friendly port. Along the way Jon Burke and his friends were amazed to find how easily they fell into comradeship with these simple Russian sailors. It seemed somehow impossible that they were citizens of an "enemy" nation. *Patriot* crew members rather reluctantly relinquished their shipwrecked companions at San Juan. The Soviet fishermen were profuse in their thanksgiving, especially to Jon, who they said "saved their lives." Jon did not mind for he had acquired another story to tell which would point up the superiority of American-made vessels over Russian.

Burke and company refueled and pointed once more toward the beau-tiful Bermudas. Midway, they picked up on their radio serious warnings about new squall formations. Before they could decide on the best course, a storm hit their starboard side with such ferocity that it felt as though they had been swatted repeatedly by the hand of the devil. There was nothing to do but pray and ride it out. By the time the tempest subsided, the *Patriot* crew was almost afraid to survey the damage. No leak was discovered, but they were dismayed upon learning that the ship's rudder mechanism had been rendered inoperable.

All they could do was to issue an S.O.S. and hope they would not be left to drift for days. Fortunately, the following day an American nuclear-powered submarine surfaced beside them and the whole *Patriot* crew was taken aboard. They were informed by the captain that the sub was headed for London and that due to the pressure of time, they could not afford to put in at any other port. Thus, Jon Burke resigned himself to being confined in the belly of a Polaris sub for at least three days. Depressed, as he lay restlessly upon his bed that night, giving silent voice to his emotions, he prayed:

"O Lord, I call to thee *out of my distress,*
    believing that thou wilt be faithful to my supplications.
For though thou hast permitted me to suffer calamity,
    yet canst thou deliver me.
Thou hast laid thine hand upon me;
like the suit of a deep-sea diver
    have I felt weighed down by it.
Here am I, *the waters closed in over me,*
    the deep was round about me.
And yet though seaweed entangle me,
    it shall be to me the enfolding arms of thee.
There are those who worship idols,
    who are more materialistic than Marxist ideology,
    who *forsake their true loyalty.*
But I, with the voice of thanksgiving,
    will sacrifice to thee.
Upon thy compelling altar
    I offer up my resistant spirit.
For at the last I know—
    Deliverance belongs to the Lord!"

Then after what seemed like many minutes, the Lord spoke in Jon's
inner ear:
    "My servant, Jonah, do not fear.
    You shall be released to do my work.
Go now to the people of Moscow;
    do not be troubled over what to say:
I will put my words into your heart."

Then suddenly the room seemed very quiet, but the warm glow lin-
gered and the certainty of the future prevailed. That night Jon Burke
slept well.

When the sub heaved to the surface at London and let Jon off at that
British capital city, he pulled out of his pocket the crumpled invitation he
had received several weeks before and wired Moscow his belated acceptance.

THE SPEECH

Three days later, Jon found himself in comfortable quarters in the
Leningrad Hotel of Moscow. He had contacted the conference officials,
and they were delighted to have him speak at their gathering. It appeared
to him that their profuse welcome revealed their belief that he would
provide some much-needed window dressing.

At any rate, he could not understand why they had invited him. At least he felt safe in Moscow—it was the last place on earth the devil would look for him! Perhaps, as had so often happened in the States, his name had been confused with John Burt, the well-known American religious pacifist. If this were so, mused Jon, the intelligence network of the Communists was not as strong as he had often claimed in his public speeches.

The Leningrad Hotel, where Jon stayed, was built in 1954 and was plush by Old World standards. However, he noticed that there were no stairways or fire escapes above the fourth floor. "What difference does it make," he thought. "This is where they house their foreign visitors—Americans, British, and the like!" He also was well aware that the doorman picked up the telephone every time he walked in and out.

It was called to Jon Burke's attention that he was to speak at 3 P.M. on the second day. The Soviet premier spoke on the first day in a special session held in Red Square. His speech before the Peace Congress represented the traditional Soviet position. It centered around several main points:

"Peaceful coexistence . . . mutual renunciation of war as a means of settling disputes . . . no surrender to the forces of aggression . . . intrigues of imperialist warmongers . . . German peace treaty . . . support to peoples fighting to free themselves from imperialist and colonial oppression . . . business cooperation with all countries . . ." The Soviet leader was given the usual extended rousing ovation.

When Jon Burke returned to his hotel later that evening, he met an American newspaperman who had just flown in from Paris. He had a copy of the *London Times* with him. A startling story commanded the whole front page of this otherwise staid publication. According to the account:

"A 100-megaton bomb accidentally exploded this morning in central Siberia. . . . It is estimated that more than 50,000 persons were killed by the blast and deadly radiation in this underpopulated area of the world. . . . Wind currents have carried radioactive fallout into northern China thus causing further tension in the Soviet-Chinese rift."

"How awful!" exclaimed Jon. "But it was bound to happen—somewhere." Amazing, he thought to himself, that the prime minister made no mention of the catastrophe. Jon went to his room and revised his speech somewhat, taking this latest development into account.

The next morning, as Jon strode through the streets of Moscow, he noticed that the people were in a very somber mood; they almost walked mechanically and seemed to be staring in the general direction of outer space. Fear and resentment were apparent in their countenances.

That afternoon Jon entered the Kremlin—which he discovered was just a group of government buildings with a red wall around them. He sought out the huge convention hall the Peace Congress used for its headquarters. It was a large auditorium; 2500 delegates and, in addition, 3500 observers and visitors, mostly Russian, were seated. The time came for him to deliver his address. As the moment approached, he recalled that passage in the Scriptures: ". . . do not be anxious beforehand what you are to say; but say whatever is given you in that hour, for it is not you who speak, but the Holy Spirit." (Mark 13:11) Jon hazily heard his name mentioned in a routine introduction, and he rose to speak. It seemed to him that at that very moment the Holy Spirit took hold of him—he found himself saying things which he had not even intended to say. His message, in brief, was as follows:

"I wish to begin by expressing my deep grief upon hearing of the tragic accident which has befallen the Soviet people. I am sure that all American citizens join with me in mourning your loss and reflecting soberly upon the proper response to this most calamitous event.

"We, the peoples of the world, can tolerate no longer an arms race which promises death as the lone victor. You and I want our children and grandchildren to have the chance to grow up and to cherish the values we uphold. This will not be possible unless we decide that those things which bind us together as men are more important than those things which divide us as nations.

"The common people of the Soviet Union surely want peace. We are well aware of their agonizing suffering during World War II—with twenty million of their citizens perishing in the struggle. We Americans have not known such loss since the time of the Civil War when more than a half million, North and South, lost their lives. The American people, I can assure you, want peace also, with all their hearts.

"We realize that there is much misunderstanding between us. We were surprised several years ago at the violent Russian reaction to the U-2 incident. Perhaps we do not fully understand the natural resentment of the Soviet Union occasioned by intrusion of her borders. For yours is a country which has known ill respect for boundaries—invaded at least once every century since A.D. 900. We Americans have suffered only one invasion of our continent in all our history—when the British occupied Washington and burned our Capitol during the War of 1812.

"Thus, we do not understand one another. And you do not realize the resentment we feel when Russian spies are discovered operating in the United States. Let us together work for a world where no one snoops on another, where no nation plots evil secretly against another, but *all* nations share their advantages and scientific developments for the blessing of all mankind.

"Ever since World War II we have not taken the problem of disarmament very seriously. Each side has attempted to secure the disarmament of the other at the point of its greatest strength. There must be concessions—concessions which are made, not to the other side, but for the sake of a concern for the security of common humanity. This latter need was made all too apparent by the lamentable event of yesterday.

"The bomb dropped on Hiroshima was only a baby—20 kiloton—yet capable of extinguishing 100,000 lives. In the last decade this bomb was replaced by the standard weapon in the arsenals of the nuclear powers —the 20-megaton H-bomb—so powerful as to be the equivalent in fire power to all the bullets shot, shells fired, and bombs dropped in all of World War II by all participants! We also have the 100-megaton weapon —and we have just seen what it can do.

"Do we, whether Christian, Communist, Buddhist, or agnostic, have the moral restraint necessary to control all of this power in our own lifetime? Let us then return to the conference table again and again. There are risks no matter what we do. In a substantial disarmament agreement the U.S. is risking the dangers involved in moving away from a defense-oriented economy. In a random on-site inspection system the U.S.S.R. risks opening up its somewhat secret society.

"But as there are dangers of loss, there are also prospects for gain. Would life not be better if there were no longer a ring of bases around the Soviet Union? Would there not be much relief in the world if no country had cause to be anxious about Russian missile-armed submarines along the Atlantic coast or Polaris subs in the Mediterranean? Would not all countries feel safer if they could be assured that no missiles were pointed in their direction from bases near or far? Would not tensions be eased if there were no military secrets to be carefully guarded—thus rendering obsolete the role of the international spy?

"As a Christian, then, in the name of Christ, I beseech you to know the blessing of being 'peacemakers,' to call your own countries to a peace that is more than a slogan or an empty word. For true peace means:

> —to work for those objectives which will serve the world's need, unconcerned about buttressing our own nation's pride;
>
> —to labor for all means of building trust and faith and confidence and to frown upon all policies that rouse suspicion;
>
> —to be willing to take the risks now lest tomorrow's world make probable our mutual annihilation.

"Today it is not the United States and the Soviet Union alone which face nuclear destruction. We are collectively threatened by a countdown on all humanity. Perhaps the count has already moved on down to ten or five. The question is: 'Will it hold there?' Can we be assured that the accident experienced yesterday will not be repeated? Or that, if such repetition occurred in any country, it would not be misinterpreted as a first-strike attack?

"Let us repent and move now into that world where swords are beat into plowshares, and spears into pruning hooks, and where atom bombs are dismantled and the power of the sun is used to benefit all mankind. *Spa-see-bah.* "*

Jon Burke left the platform in somewhat of a daze. He felt as though he had just spoken in tongues. Not a page of the manuscript he brought with him had been turned. He recalled the silence and then what sounded to him like polite applause as he left the hall and headed back to his hotel room. He had a headache and could hardly remember anything of what he had said.

THE AFTERMATH

His plane was due out in two hours—so he had time only to pack and ride out to the Moscow airport. He had no customs problem because he had made no purchases—since he was thoroughly convinced that the Russians had nothing worth buying. He spent a few kopeks for a glass of milk which helped him to gain a few hours of sleep on the airliner to East Berlin. As the airport bus rolled into West Berlin, the passengers let out a cheer, and Jon felt very much like squatting down and kissing the precious free soil.

Jon rose early from a good night's sleep and went to the lobby to purchase an English language newspaper. The headlines which captured his eyes seemed unbelievable: AMERICAN LAUNCHES PEACE BREAKTHROUGH! RUSSIANS SHOW CHANGE OF HEART. A two-column wire dispatch flanked by pictures told the story:

> Well-known American anti-Communist Jon Burke proved the catalytic agent which launched the greatest demonstration seen in Moscow since the days of the October Revolution in 1917.
>
> Burke, speaking passionately before a session of the Moscow Peace Congress, called for a halt to the arms race. He challenged the Soviet Union to make new attempts at a substantial disarmament agreement. His address was delivered against the backdrop of the previous day's sobering event—the accidental explosion of a 100-megaton bomb in Siberia.
>
> The full impact of Mr. Burke's speech began to be felt late yesterday afternoon and evening as the news of its message swept rapidly through the capital city by word of mouth. Spontaneously crowds

*"Thank you" in Russian.

began to gather in Red Square until more than a million people had assembled in that area. The Muscovites were in a high emotional pitch which seemed to be motivated at once by fear, resentment, and desperate hope. They began to chant in unison: "Mir! Mir! Mir!"* So lusty were these resounding shouts it seemed that the adjacent Kremlin walls would come tumbling down. The people were extremely overwrought: men raised their fists; many women knelt to pray with tears running down their cheeks.

After almost two hours of demonstrations, the prime minister walked from the Kremlin area and mounted the platform at the Lenin mausoleum. He publicly and informally promised the people two things: (1) the following day would be declared a national day of mourning; (2) the government would speedily take the practical steps necessary to reach a disarmament agreement with the United States.

The Kremlin subsequently released to the press the text of a telegram sent by the Soviet premier to the President of the United States. The text read as follows:

"My esteemed Mr. President:
In the light of the most tragic event of recent days for the future welfare of humankind, the Soviet Union requests that disarmament negotiators reconvene immediately at Geneva. We are pleased to announce in advance that the U.S.S.R. will accept any reasonable inspection plan agreed upon by the unaligned states.

                                        Premier of the U.S.S.R."

What Jon Burke read angered him. How could these Communists warmongers who are out to "bury us" sincerely want peace? Were they not demons damned by God? How dare they pretend to repent!

He went to his room and wept. "And to think," he sobbed, "that I had something to do with all of this! God, forgive me!" Later that morning a group of reporters came to his room for an interview. They found him unshaven, red-eyed, somewhat incoherent. He sat on the edge of the bed clutching the newspaper in one hand and his Burke Society card in the other. Great tears fell upon the membership card. All he could say was, "My God, what have I done!"

Even the most zealous of the reporters decided it was the wrong time for an interview and regretfully departed.

In the early afternoon Jon decided to go for a walk. The sky had darkened and a foggy drizzle turned pedestrians to plodding silhouettes.

*"Peace."

Jon was oblivious to all; but at one corner he stopped before the open door of a church. By the soft light that outlined the chancel he saw that the church was vacant. He went in—for it was not uncommon for him to turn to the church in the dark moments of his life.

At the chancel he prostrated himself before the altar and prayed fervently: "I beseech thee, O Lord, *is not this what I said when I was yet in my country?* I knew that it was wrong for me to undertake this mission. That is why I tried to get away from it all through the sea cruise. *For I knew that thou art a gracious God and merciful, slow to anger, and abounding in steadfast love . . . Therefore now, O Lord, take my life from me, I beseech thee, for it is better for me to die than to live."*

He pressed his throbbing forehead against the cool marble communion rail for what seemed like a long time. Then he felt something quivering and wet at his side. Startled, he looked down to see a small nondescript dog which had wandered into the refuge of the sanctuary. The animal was shivering uncontrollably and was so wet that his clinging fur shrank his body to grotesque proportions. "Poor thing," said Jon sympathetically, "I understand just how you feel." Almost instinctively Jon took out his clean handkerchief and began wiping the dog dry. When this proved insufficient, he took off his white silk scarf (for it was chilly that day) and began to use it as a towel.

But this temporary diversion was not enough for Jon to overcome his persistent state of emotional travail. With the befriended pup at his side, he turned once more to airing his grievance before God: "Lord, O Lord, what have I done! What will happen to my crusade now? How can we keep the people alerted to creeping Communism? What will happen to my defense business? I wish I were dead!"

Suddenly he felt the mysterious presence of some third Being. In a voice strangely familiar but always surprising to him, he heard these words: "Jonah, Jonah—*Do you do well to be angry?"*

"Yes, Lord," said Jon, "I am *angry enough to die."*

"Why, Jonah, why? Do you remember? You had mercy upon the Russian fishermen; you also had pity upon this poor mongrel, which is here tonight and wandering the streets tomorrow. Therefore, should I not have pity upon Moscow, *that great city, in which there are more than a hundred and twenty thousand* infants *who do not know their right hand from their left,* and also some dogs?"

V | * MICAH

*All material in this part is new in this edition

Micah—His Times and Ours

Micah was born at Mareshah, a village located in the southwest part of Palestine, not far from the Philistine city of Gath. Mareshah was a small frontier town very much exposed to potential attack from either the Philistines to the west or the Egyptians to the south. Micah, as he expressed international concern, was deeply fearful of invasion of his beloved village and, as a result, generally favored a peaceful stance for the kingdom of Judah.

We do not know if Micah ever met Amos, but as he lived only twenty miles from Tekoa, home of that prophet, it is quite likely that he knew of Amos and was considerably influenced by his spirit and teachings. Unlike his contemporary, First Isaiah, who was an aristocrat, Jerusalem-bred, and a familiar figure at the royal court, Micah was a small town artisan with little education and no connections.

Micah must have lived between 737 to 686 B.C. since there are references to his prophecy occuring during the reigns in Judah of Jotham, Ahaz, and Hezekiah (1:1). Assyria, the dominant nation of the period, had conquered Syria (732 B.C.) and Israel (722 B.C.) to the north and was now menacing Judah which, as a buffer state, seemed to be a minor impediment to her conquest of Egypt. The major international crisis of the period was the invasion by King Sennacherib of Assyria in 701, a time in which Micah warns Hezekiah that Zion will be "plowed as a field" and Jerusalem shall "become a heap of ruins." (3:12)

Micah saw his own native town, a crossroads between Assyrian and Egyptian conflict, coming to utter destruction in the event of open warfare. Therefore, he was fearful of any armies on the march and advocated a peaceful settlement and trust in the Lord.

Since Jeremiah, in the 26th chapter of his book, refers to Micah prophesying in the days of Hezekiah and we have references to Sennacherib's invasion, this tends to limit the prophet's public ministry to between 714 and 700 B.C.

Morals were disgustingly low in Micah's day. Corruption abounded among government officials. The nation was internally soft and weak and vulnerable to conquest. Micah believed that Judah's best defense lay in strengthening its moral underpinnings.

Hezekiah was one of Judah's best kings in terms of ethical and religious sensitivity. He seemed to be receptive to the prophetic utterances of Isaiah and Micah. In fact, Jeremiah gives Micah considerable credit for having caused King Hezekiah to "fear the LORD and entreat the favor of the LORD." (Jer. 26:19) It may have been partly in response to the harshly critical prophecies of Micah that Hezekiah initiated a vigorous reform movement demolishing the images worshiped by the cults and even by some believers in Yahweh. Although Hezekiah implemented an outward reform movement, still he was singularly unsuccessful as leader in setting a moral tone during his reign which had any effect upon the ethical practices of the people of Judah.

THE MAJOR TEACHINGS OF MICAH

It is commonly accepted that the prophet Micah did not write the entire book appearing under his name and that most likely at least chapters 4 and 5 represent collections added to the book as later supplements. Therefore, "a manuscript, such as the present text of Micah, consisted of the basic document plus the comments which accrued to it during the time it circulated as a living growing book."[1] (This was probably between 700 and 200 B.C.) In other words, the prophet was "paraphrased" for 500 years and by about 200 B.C. the book became considered as holy Scripture. For the purposes of this volume, since all other possible authors remain unknown, we shall refer to the teachings found in the book as utterances of Micah.

Early on, Micah was told by the leaders of Judah: " 'Do not preach . . . one should not preach of such things; disgrace will not overtake us.' " (2:6) In effect they were saying: don't pronounce your words of judgment; we aren't going to come to disgrace as you say we are. This was the same kind of counsel that Amos had received earlier in Israel when they told him to "never again prophesy at Bethel" (Amos 7:13) but go back to Judah and preach. With Micah, as with Amos, such self-serving advice fell on deaf ears.

What put Micah into conflict with his contemporaries was that he was a "prime hater," as Mary Ellen Chase points out: "He hated cities, even Jerusalem, the capital city of his country. . . . He hated the Assyrians. He hated the rich. And, above all else, he hated the wrongs committed by men against their fellows. His brief book . . . flames with righteous hatred, with justified fury and condemnation."[2]

Undoubtedly the preaching that got Micah into the most trouble dealt specifically with the wrongdoing of the powerful leaders of government, religion, and commerce. These people should have known better, but they didn't. They were insensitive and obsessed with their own power and greed. Judah was faced with a "leadership crisis." The very people its citizens should have been able to turn to for help—government leaders, priests, prophets—were corrupt.

> Its heads give judgment for a bribe,
>   its priests teach for hire,
>   its prophets divine for money. (3:11)

The wealthy landholders of Jerusalem and leaders of commerce in general come under sharp rebuke from the tongue of Micah. He warns:

> Woe to those who devise wickedness
>   and work evil upon their beds!
> When the morning dawns, they perform it,
>   because it is in the power of their hand.
> They covet fields, and seize them,
>   and houses, and take them away;
> they oppress a man and his house,
>   a man and his inheritance. (2:1, 2)

Again, at the beginning of the third chapter of Micah, the prophet rails against the "rulers of the house of Israel!" (3:1) If anyone should know justice, they should know it, but they do not. Instead, they hate the good and love evil. Then, in very specific and terrifying language Micah depicts the uncaring exploitive treatment of their people by government officials. Not only do the leaders destroy their citizens by their poor example, and exploitive acts, but when they are through with their victims, they are good for nothing but a pot of stew!

Micah concludes the section by stating that what happens to the nation then is not due to intervention of the vengeance of God, but the direct result of the sins of Judah's lamentable leadership. Micah says:

> Therefore because of you
>   Zion shall be plowed as a field;
> Jerusalem shall become a heap of ruins,
>   And the mountain of the house a wooded height. (3:12)

Micah places the fault squarely where it belongs—upon the failure of leadership.

Another important teaching of Micah may be found in his lashing out at the false prophets. Instead of providing guidance, they led people astray. They cry " 'Peace' " when they have something to eat, said Micah, but "declare war against him who puts nothing into their mouths." (3:5) In other words, as long as their own economic interests were served they spoke approvingly of their benefactors.

As Rolland Wolfe characterized it so well: "Instead of an agency of

human uplift, religion in Micah's day was becoming a system of racketeer-
ing carried on by unscrupulous prophetic professionals for personal
profit."[3]

As a result of this materialistic outlook, Micah said: "The sun shall go
down upon the prophets." (3:6) They would have no vision, be disgraced,
be put to shame.

Another major teaching of Micah centers around specific social sins
and impending judgment. He recounts this in 6:9–16. Micah begins by
saying it isn't himself the prophet speaking but "the voice of the LORD
cries to the city." (6:9) He calls upon the people to hear it. Some scholars
believe that this section was delivered directly after the terrible siege of
Jerusalem by Sennacherib in 701 B.C. following the devastation of much
of Judah. Fortunately for the capital city the attacking Assyrian troops
were suddenly called away and the siege was lifted. One might think that
this would have been a propitious time for Micah to speak with the
expectation of a receptive audience.

In the name of God, he railed against corrupt mercantile practices—
the treasures which they hoarded in gathering loot from the poor, the use
of scant measures, scales that shortchanged customers, weights which did
not balance as much as they were supposed to. Violence, lies, and deceit
were everywhere.

For this, the people of Jerusalem would be judged. Assyria would attack
again and take them into exile. It would not be a happy time. They would
have something to eat but never enough to satisfy. Their stomachs would
groan with gnawing hunger. Their captors would reap everything they
had sown. As Dr. Wolfe summarizes it: " . . . the grain they were about
to sow would be reaped by the enemy. The olive oil they were about to
extract would be used by the Assyrians. The wine they were about to
press would be drunk by their conquerors. . . . "[4]

Micah's oracle ends with the implication that, except for a sudden
repentance, catastrophe would befall Judah, the object of desolation,
hissing, and scorn rendered by other nations.

It is a dismal picture, but it is not the end. For God is not one who
would "retain his anger forever." In the closing psalm (7:18–20) Micah
(or his interpreter) depicts Yahweh as granting special providence for the
"remnant of his inheritance"(7:18)—for those left of his chosen ones
after they pass through ordeal. The Lord pardons their iniquity and
passes over their transgression. His fundamental character is revealed,
for "he delights in steadfast love." (7:18) His "compassion" reigns supreme as his people's iniquities are forgotten and their sins cast far from
him—"into the depths of the sea." (7:19) God's relationship to the people of Judah will be one of "faithfulness" and "steadfast love," thus

fulfilling the ultimate promise to their forefathers in "the days of old." (7:20)

Hope is the last word of the prophet, as Harold Bosley notes—"hope which . . . is born of faith in God and in his love of man."[5]

MICAH'S MESSAGE FOR THE MODERN ERA

Micah clearly saw in his day that there was a *leadership crisis*. Of the leaders of government he said: "Hear, you heads of Jacob and rulers of the house of Israel! Is it not for you to know justice?" (3:1) He was saying: you, of all people, should know better. But instead you "tear the skin from off my people, and their flesh from off their bones; . . . and chop them up like meat in a kettle." (3:2, 3)

During the Watergate period we saw those who were to set the example for the nation—those who talked incessantly about "law and order," in fact were breaking the law—approving illegal break-ins, sanctioning burglaries, ordering lawless wiretaps, abusing power by authorizing IRS audits on lists of "enemies." In a democracy it is essential that those at the top do not put themselves above the law, in a position where the laws of the nation do not apply to the powerful, but only to the common man. As engraved on the front of the U.S. Supreme Court building, there must be *"equal* justice under law."

The leadership crisis extended in Micah's time to others who were needed to, and should have been expected to, set the moral tone for Judah. Government leaders and judges were corrupt; priests taught the faith to those who could pay them, and prophets tempered their "oracles" so as to please the ears of the rich and powerful. Those who could have provided guidance to a straying people were actually blind guides and babbling voices.

We are living in an era when a federal judge was convicted and served a prison sentence; when a U.S. Supreme Court justice stepped down under accusations of conflict of interest. In our capitalistic society the reputation of business continues to be at the lowest ebb. Major corporations have paid bribes to representatives abroad; executives have made illegal political contributions out of company funds; a major insurance firm has deceived the public about its assets and profits, turning its conglomerate into a computerized shell.

In our current period there is no recognized prophetic voice raised to tell the people what they need to know. The age of "great preachers" is over. Since Martin Luther King's death, no representative of the clergy has emerged as a compassionate advocate of urgent social change. The Fosdicks, the Niebuhrs, the Bosleys, the John Bennetts, the Abraham Heschels, and the Martin Luther Kings are gone from the public plat-

form. As St. Paul once said: "How are they to hear without a preacher?"
(Rom. 10:14)

How pertinent Micah was when he said: "If a man should go about and
utter wind and lies, saying, 'I will preach to you of wine and strong drink,'
he would be preacher for this people!" (2:11) How often congregations
would like their preachers to rail against someone else's sin—like that of
the alcoholic—while they remain comfortably unperturbed, spared from
any talk about personal life-style, an Equal Rights Amendment, the needs
of street persons in Calcutta, or making peace with the North Vietnamese.

Church leaders should not typify ecclesiastical government by Gallup;
leaders should lead, clarify the issues, point the way. Religious officials
should constantly evaluate whether or not they have turned over the
prophetic function to politicians; whether or not ethical perspectives are
being brought to bear on the making of policies under which all of God's
children in America are going to have to live.

Micah brings us a further message when he clearly enunciates *what God
wants ultimately from his people—justice, kindness, and humility.* Perhaps
Micah's most famous teaching for then and now is found in his rhetorical
question: "What does the LORD require of you but to do justice, and to
love kindness, and to walk humbly with your God?" (6:8)

The justice would be reflected in fair-minded landlords, in responsible
and non-exploitive leaders, in merchants who use true scales. Kindness
would be found in the way in which brother treats brother, the steadfast
love of God bringing forth acts of compassion among the people. Humility would come as Judah's land was ravished, her population decimated,
and in desperation she turned once more to the Lord.

Exercising justice in today's world is no simple matter. Corporations
will need to understand that it is even in their own best interests to treat
both employees and customers fairly, to really care about the well-being
of their workers, and to meet product and pricing standards in serving
the interests of consumers. Professional people will need to concentrate
on the service they can perform rather than the fees they can extract.
Government civil servants will have to reassess their working day in terms
of the public interest and taxpayers receiving benefits through their
efforts. Factory workers will need to feel they are producing something
useful and not just driving a rivet, turning a screw, or drilling a hole.

Being kind in our society has become much more than just offering a
glass of water with a smile. In many cases it means knowing when to keep
silent, or going out of your way to express concern for people in need,
or showing you care about persons who are under attack.

A preacher from Georgia wrote a letter of consolation a few years ago
to a high government official who was fired following a personal scandal.

The minister had been in Washington at the time the firing took place and he felt exceedingly sorry for the man and his family. So, although he did not know the high official, he wrote a pastoral-type letter to him. A few weeks later an answer came back. The man wrote: "I've been carrying your letter around with me in my pocket and I take it out and read it occasionally. It is hard for me to tell you how much your letter has meant to me and my family. I, too, believe that God cares and, with his help, I can begin a new life. Thanks so very much." Simple kindness.

Walking humbly is perhaps the most difficult of virtues. This becomes increasingly true as you move up the ladder of success and have so many people telling you how good you are. Perhaps the only way any person of achievement can be humble is to "walk . . . with . . . God." When you compare your creativity with the Creator, your power with the Omnipotent, and your love with the love of Christ, only then can you or I move in meekness.

Another cue for our current era can be found in Micah's counsel concerning peace. In effect, he said that *peace will come when we create a world in which "none shall make them afraid."* It is a great ideal. If Micah's prophecy is correct then we need to move toward a world where:

> They shall beat their swords into plowshares,
>   and their spears into pruning hooks;
> nation shall not lift up sword against nation,
>   neither shall they learn war any more;
> but they shall sit every man under his vine and under his fig tree,
>   and none shall make them afraid. . . . (4:3, 4)

It is hard to build a world where the weak are not pawns before the strong. Charles DeVisscher once said: "A regime founded on oppression is by the unlimited scope of its powers a threat to peace in the external sphere as it is to liberty within the country."[6] Human rights are an important aspect of any world where we expect men and women to sit peacefully under their own fig tree.

The trend in the world today is toward dictatorship. It is depressing to contemplate that most of the nations of Latin America, Africa, and Asia are under authoritarian rule. Such regimes are bound by fiat decree to make some decent people "afraid." What a tragedy! What a heritage we have left in the wake of our arms assistance programs and our training of military personnel! Did we share our Constitution with them? Our Bill of Rights? Did we train them in the precepts of human liberty?

It is difficult to imagine that any great world power could dominate the world and not fundamentally make its client states afraid. Could the Soviet Union? Could China? Could the United States? No, probably not even our United States. Because as power is acquired by a country, the national character of that state takes on pride. It believes it can do no wrong. Success proves to itself its own infallibility. The nation falls prey to arrogance.

Probably no nation or combination of nations have enough restraint and objectivity to build by themselves an international community which will be sufficient to maintain true peace. Only a world community which has within its authority and power the capability of keeping nations from war, settling disputes, providing for peaceful change and guaranteeing personal human rights will be competent for the task before us. This may mean limited world government and the surrender by nations of the sovereign right to make war. But it is hard to imagine any other way where none shall make nations and peoples afraid.

In that day, "the nations shall . . . be ashamed of all their might" (7:16) and beat their swords into plowshares and never learn war any more.

Selections from Micah

Woe to those who devise wickedness
  and work evil upon their beds!
When the morning dawns, they perform it,
  because it is in the power of their hand.
They covet fields, and seize them;
  and houses, and take them away;
they oppress a man and his house,
  a man and his inheritance.
Therefore thus says the LORD:
Behold, against this family I am devising evil,
  from which you cannot remove your necks;
and you shall not walk haughtily,
  for it will be an evil time.
In that day they shall take up a taunt song against you,
  and wail with bitter lamentation,
and say, "We are utterly ruined;
  he changes the portion of my people;
how he removes it from me!
  Among our captors he divides our fields."
Therefore you will have none to cast the line by lot
  in the assembly of the LORD.

And I said:
Hear, you heads of Jacob
  and rulers of the house of Israel!
Is it not for you to know justice?—
  you who hate the good and love the evil,
who tear the skin from off my people,
  and their flesh from off their bones;
who eat the flesh of my people,
  and flay their skin from off them,
and break their bones in pieces,
  and chop them up like meat in a kettle,

like flesh in a caldron.
Then they will cry to the LORD,
  but he will not answer them;
he will hide his face from them at that time,
  because they have made their deeds evil.

THE PROPHETS LEAD PEOPLE ASTRAY 3:5–8

Thus says the LORD concerning the prophets
  who lead my people astray,
who cry "Peace"
  when they have something to eat,
but declare war against him
  who puts nothing into their mouths.
Therefore it shall be night to you, without vision,
  and darkness to you, without divination.
The sun shall go down upon the prophets,
  and the day shall be black over them;
the seers shall be disgraced,
  and the diviners put to shame;
they shall all cover their lips,
  for there is no answer from God.
But as for me, I am filled with power,
  with the Spirit of the LORD,
  and with justice and might,
to declare to Jacob his transgression
  and to Israel his sin.

ZION SHALL BE PLOWED AS A FIELD 3:9–12

Hear this, you heads of the house of Jacob
  and rulers of the house of Israel,
who abhor justice
  and pervert all equity,
who build Zion with blood
  and Jerusalem with wrong.
Its heads give judgment for a bribe,
  its priests teach for hire,
  its prophets divine for money;
yet they lean upon the LORD and say,
  "Is not the LORD in the midst of us?
  No evil shall come upon us."
Therefore because of you

Zion shall be plowed as a field;
Jerusalem shall become a heap of ruins,
   and the mountain of the house a wooded height.

SWORDS INTO PLOWSHARES 4:1–4

It shall come to pass in the latter days
   that the mountain of the house of the Lord
shall be established as the highest of the mountains,
   and shall be raised up above the hills;
and peoples shall flow to it,
   and many nations shall come, and say:
"Come, let us go up to the mountain of the Lord,
   to the house of the God of Jacob;
that he may teach us his ways
   and we may walk in his paths."
For out of Zion shall go forth the law,
   and the word of the Lord from Jerusalem.
He shall judge between many peoples,
   and shall decide for strong nations afar off;
and they shall beat their swords into plowshares,
   and their spears into pruning hooks;
nation shall not lift up sword against nation,
   neither shall they learn war any more;
but they shall sit every man under his vine and under his fig tree,
   and none shall make them afraid;
   for the mouth of the Lord of hosts has spoken.

DESTRUCTION TO DISOBEDIENT NATIONS 5:10–15

And in that day, says the Lord,
   I will cut off your horses from among you
   and will destroy your chariots;
and I will cut off the cities of your land
   and throw down all your strongholds;
and I will cut off sorceries from your hand,
   and you shall have no more soothsayers;
and I will cut off your images
   and your pillars from among you,
and you shall bow down no more
   to the work of your hands;
and I will root out your Asherim from among you
   and destroy your cities.

And in anger and wrath I will execute vengeance
  upon the nations that did not obey.

WHAT THE LORD REQUIRES 6:6–8

"With what shall I come before the LORD,
  and bow myself before God on high?
Shall I come before him with burnt offerings,
  with calves a year old?
Will the LORD be pleased with thousands of rams,
  with ten thousands of rivers of oil?
Shall I give my first-born for my transgression,
  the fruit of my body for the sin of my soul?"
He has showed you, O man, what is good;
  and what does the LORD require of you
but to do justice, and to love kindness,
  and to walk humbly with your God?

RICH MEN FULL OF VIOLENCE 6:10–15

Can I forget the treasures of wickedness in the house of the wicked
  and the scant measure that is accursed?
Shall I acquit the man with wicked scales
  and with a bag of deceitful weights?
Your rich men are full of violence;
  your inhabitants speak lies,
  and their tongue is deceitful in their mouth.
Therefore I have begun to smite you,
  making you desolate because of your sins.
You shall eat, but not be satisfied,
  and there shall be hunger in your inward parts;
you shall put away, but not save,
  and what you save I will give to the sword.
You shall sow, but not reap;
you shall tread olives, but not anoint
  yourselves with oil;
you shall tread grapes, but not drink wine.

ENEMIES IN ONE'S OWN HOUSE 7:2–7

The godly man has perished from the earth,
  and there is none upright among men;
they all lie in wait for blood,
  and each hunts his brother with a net.

Their hands are upon what is evil, to do it diligently;
   the prince and the judge ask for a bribe,
and the great man utters the evil desire of his soul;
   thus they weave it together.
The best of them is like a brier,
   the most upright of them a thorn hedge.
The day of their watchmen, of their punishment, has come;
   now their confusion is at hand.
Put no trust in a neighbor,
   have no confidence in a friend;
guard the doors of your mouth
   from her who lies in your bosom;
for the son treats the father with contempt,
   the daughter rises up against her mother,
   the daughter-in-law against her mother-in-law;
   a man's enemies are the men of his own house.
But as for me, I will look to the LORD,
   I will wait for the God of my salvation;
   my God will hear me.

NATIONS ASHAMED OF THEIR MIGHT 7:16, 17

The nations shall see and be ashamed of
   all their might;
they shall lay their hands on their mouths;
   their ears shall be deaf;
they shall lick the dust like a serpent,
   like the crawling things of the earth;
they shall come trembling out of their strongholds,
   they shall turn in dread to the LORD our God,
   and they shall fear because of thee.

GOD DELIGHTS IN STEADFAST LOVE 7:18–20

Who is a God like thee, pardoning iniquity
   and passing over transgression
   for the remnant of his inheritance?
He does not retain his anger for ever
   because he delights in steadfast love.
He will again have compassion upon us,
   he will tread our iniquities under foot.
Thou wilt cast all our sins
   into the depths of the sea.

Thou wilt show faithfulness to Jacob
   and steadfast love to Abraham,
as thou hast sworn to our fathers
   from the days of old.

Micah—Voice of the Lord on Social Sin

THE CORRUPTION OF POWER (2:1)

Woe to those who devise wickedness
and work evil upon their beds!
When the morning dawns, they perform it,
because it is in the power of their hand.
He was innocent and naive
his mind was well-intentioned
and his heart well-motivated.
He was elected to the U.S. Congress
and came to serve the public good.
But on the first day he took office
he determined his prime objective:
above all, stay in power.
After all, who can serve the District better?
who loves my people more?
And so he began to do what the job required.
He surrounded himself with "yes" men and attractive women,
all from the home district,
whose jobs depended on his remaining in the House.
They all had large families "back home"
and were useful instruments in future campaigns.
They answered most correspondence with form letters
run off with autotype equipment.
An occasional note of personal regards
was penned at the bottom—with a rubber stamp!
The Congressman was frank to admit
his generous use of the franking privilege
through which he could send periodic reports,
press releases, and bulletins
to inform his constituency (at public expense)
of all the good he was doing for them:
the bills that he was co-sponsoring
(which he had never read),
the public works projects he had supported
which brought largesse to the District,
the public interest legislation pressed,

giving jobs and income to people in his county,
and, at the same time, how he had opposed
   increases in taxes by a wasteful bureaucracy!
Visitors to Washington from his hometown base
   were given the VIP treatment and hospitality
   charged to a miscellaneous account
   they would pay taxes for.
Others calling from special interest groups
   were also most cordially received,
especially if they made known
   their campaign fund coffers
   were open to all who voted "right."
He went to the cocktail parties
   of the groups with greatest influence
in the company of his most attractive secretary,
   who was good at watering plants.
And as time went by,
   being a Representative was more enjoyable
   than representing human beings.

HOUSING

They covet fields, and seize them;
   and houses, and take them away.
Woe unto the slumlords
   who buy apartments and never repair them,
   who, through accelerated depreciation, turn a quick profit every few
      years,
   but meanwhile let their properties crumble and decay, destroying their
      inhabitants.
And you wonder why your public housing fails:
mothers have to leave the bedroom lights on at night
   to keep the rats from biting their children.
When door knobs fall off, no one can fix them,
   and when refrigerators freeze up, no one knows how to defrost.
There is no child care,
   so mothers cannot go out to work.
There is no employment bureau,
   so the jobless hang around the project and find mischief to perform.
There is no security force,
   so the residents fear for their lives.
There are no counseling services,
   so no one has help with problems.

There is no tenant organization,
  so no one feels responsible for keeping things up.
And so the government must buy back its own mortgages,
because it underfinanced the project in the first place,
and left the sponsor dangling from a piece of bureaucratic red tape.
And thus HUD wins the prize
  as the biggest slumlord of them all!

WHAT IS GOOD (6:6, 8)

"With what shall I come before the Lord
  and bow myself before God on high?"
I shall attend church regularly dressed in my best suit, occasionally
    ushering and passing the plate.
  Accept my offering, O God.
I shall dangle from my lapel twenty years of perfect attendance at Sunday
    School.
I shall own and use a special Bible in the "original" King James, red
    lettered, gilt edged, Morocco bound, printed on India paper.
I shall rise early each morning to receive the sacraments from a yawning
    priest.
Receive my religiousness, O Lord.
I shall have my children baptized in the church,
  insist on their participation in church school,
  fulfill my obligation by seeing that they are confirmed by the pastor,
I shall attend weekly prayer breakfasts
  where men are warmed by coffee and good fellowship
  as much as by the power of the Holy Spirit.
I shall pay five dollars a week to the church even though I miss it,
And contribute ten hymnals to the sanctuary appeal in the name of my
    dear departed mother.
I shall teach a class of antsy junior highs on Sunday morning, diligently
    taking my turn in the transmission of the holy faith.
Receive my commitment, O God.
I shall serve on the Board of Trustees, the Finance Committee, and the
    Membership Commission,
I shall arrange flowers on the altar, light the candles, and serve as
    communion steward.
Remember my devotion, Almighty God.
He has showed you, O man, [and O woman] *what is good;*
  and what does the Lord require of you,
but to do justice, and to love kindness,
  and to walk humbly with your God?

WIRETAPPING (7:5)

Put no trust in a neighbor,
  have no confidence in a friend;
guard the doors of your mouth
  from her who lies in your bosom.

For the day is coming when every family will be listening to the
    conversations of every other family.

When every business wiretaps its competitors,

and the government places all its citizens under surveillance.

But the government doesn't trust itself,

for each agency records the doings of sister agencies,

and we have run out of secretaries to type from the tapes,
  and the tapes are piling up,
  and the typescripts remain unfiled,

and the bureaucracy is like the community where everybody earned a
    living by taking in everyone else's dirty laundry,

and that community ran out of water and soap,

And no one knew how to do anything except wash clothes.

Why do you delight in making people afraid?

You do it all in the name of freedom,
  of trapping the mafia and spying on enemy agents,
  and of breaking the back of organized crime,

but you are breaking our backs!

Your people are afraid to talk to one another,

for fear what they say will be misinterpreted,
  so it is better not to talk.

You say: why should they care if they are overheard?
  They should have nothing to hide!

But conversations become more guarded
  and people do not speak their mind,

For they believe everything they say may be reported, pieced together,
    garbled, and misinterpreted,

and so this becomes a silent nation, full of whispers and shrugs of the
    shoulder.

No one voices an honest opinion
  or ventures a thought
  or thinks out loud.

And thus your security has not saved the nation, but destroyed it,
  and produced a paranoid people,
    where the wiretappers are being wiretapped,
    and the conversations recorded have all become innocuous,

the time of day, the weather, the colors of autumn,
rendered by citizens in funereal tones.

NONE SHALL MAKE THEM AFRAID (7:16; 4:3, 4)

The nations shall see
   and be ashamed of all their might.
They shall see themselves
   placing crippling tax burdens upon their own people.
   See, and be ashamed.
They shall see malnourished children of the world,
   not fed with bread, because of the cost of bombs.
   See, and be ashamed.
They shall see defense workers who so covet their jobs
   they would rather produce obsolete weapons
   than risk converting plants to mass transit, modular housing, or solar
      energy.
   See, and be ashamed.
They shall see developing nations
   buying expensive arms when their own children in arms need better
      health care and nutrition,
   purchasing defense materials when their own people need defense
      against smallpox, rickets, and illiteracy,
   ordering weapons of war, when their citizens need weapons to fight
      disease, ignorance, and starvation,
   needing penicillin, books, and farming tools.
   See, and be ashamed.
They shall see the richer nations selling their military wares to the poorer
      countries
   whose people don't have a decent diet or enough schools, or sufficient
      physicians.
   See, and be ashamed.
They shall see the great powers
   competing with one another for superior advantage:
   who will make the biggest bomb?
   who will place more warheads on the tip of a missile?
   who will excel in overkill capacity?
   See, and be ashamed.
They shall see the United States spending huge amounts of its income
      on the military,
   while it postpones national health care, welfare reform, and jobs
      programs,
   until "adequate funds" are available.

See, and be ashamed.
The day will come when all *the nations shall see*
  and be ashamed of . . . their might,
and they shall beat their swords into plowshares,
  and their spears into pruning hooks;
nation shall not lift up sword against nation,
  neither shall they learn war any more;
but they shall sit every person *under his vine and under his fig tree,*
  and none shall make them afraid.

THE STEADFAST LOVE OF GOD (7:18)

Who is a God like thee, pardoning iniquity
  and passing over transgression . . . ?
He does not retain his anger for ever
  because he delights in steadfast love.
I ate junk food yet suffered no indigestion.
I jogged once a month but flabby muscles still served me well.
I left all the lights in the house burning,
  but escaped arrest for ignoring the energy crisis.
I remembered my wife's birthday three days following,
  but she continued to live with me.
I failed to water the lawn,
  yet it kept growing green,
I was cross with my co-workers,
  but they were tolerant of my temper.
I silently cursed,
  but the Lord did not take me seriously.
Guilt tossed me through a sleepless night,
  yet the birds were still singing in the morning.
I coveted but did not steal,
  angered but did not murder,
  lusted but did not commit adultery.
Happy circumstances kept me out of jail.
I read the Holy Scriptures
  which brought me under grace instead of judgment.
I was oppressed by things undone
  but walked out into the sunlight,
  felt the caressing breeze blow away my cares,
  strolled through the park and inhaled nature's fragrance,
  absorbed the bounteous beauty of grass, bush, and tree
  and said to the world: God still loves me.

NIGHT ON CAPITOL HILL

Standing on a winter eve, from this corner can be seen
  with panoramic vision, what makes America stay green.
On one side shines the Capitol dome, gleaming white,
  seat of government, symbol of free discussion, liberty.
On the other, more dimly lit, stands the Supreme Court,
its mighty pillars outlined against murky portico,
  upon its pediment the words "Equal justice under law."
Across the street the Methodist Building stands dark,
  its chapel light glowing softly in the night.

All three are needed for democracy to work:
  true liberty, equal justice, concerned religion.
For liberty without justice leaves men free
—to exploit each other,
and justice without liberty provides "fair treatment"
—by some tyrant's rules.
But religion can give liberty a conscience,
  and justice some standards
    and the nation a purpose for its life.

VI | JEREMIAH

*This indicates new material in this edition

Vision of the Floating Tower of Babel
Christianity—Leaven or Lump?
*Policies and Practices (10:23, 24)
Prisoner of Pomposity (13:15–17)
God Looketh Upon the Heart (13:23)
The Faithful Spiritual Leader (14:14)
Backward Progress (15:5, 6)
Wars Remembered
Lonely Truth (15:16, 15, 17)
How the Wicked Prosper (12:1–2; 17:10)
The Arms Race (21:8)
Faith for the New World
The False Prophets (23:13–40)
Concerning the Peace Corps

*SAINT FRANCIS

Jeremiah—His Times and Ours

THE LIFE AND TIMES OF JEREMIAH

Jeremiah, trained as a priest in the tradition of his family, was called as a young man to be "a prophet to the nations." Although he protested, "I am only a youth," he was assured of the Lord's sustaining strength.

It was a difficult time in which to preach. Under the influence of Judah's King Manasseh (687–642 B.C.), who was an Assyrian puppet, religious decadence had set in. The temple had been closed; there was no formal worship of Yahweh.

The prophet proclaimed that Judah had deserted Yahweh, "the fountain of living waters." The nation had turned to false gods which were like broken cisterns, unable to hold water. Jeremiah had searched the streets of Jerusalem in vain to find even one man "who does justice and seeks truth" so that Judah might lay claim to pardon.

In 626 B.C., the year of Jeremiah's call, King Josiah came to power. Under the leadership of the good king, the temple at Jerusalem was repaired in 622 B.C. While this rebuilding project was in progress, the workmen chanced upon a scroll hidden in the walls. The document set forth specific laws by which the nation was expected to live. Basing their action on those laws, the king and his princes immediately launched a reform movement which forbade the worship of any other gods but Yahweh. All worship was to be restricted henceforth to the temple at Jerusalem. Justice was required in all human relationships.

It soon became clear, however, that the reform largely took the direction of nationalism, and Jeremiah was keenly disappointed. The changes which were initiated, instead of purging the soul of the nation, were largely superficial. Although the altars and pillars erected to pagan gods on every high hill were destroyed and temple ritual was now rigorously observed, there was no fundamental improvement in the life of the people. To make matters worse, the religious leaders supporting the movement saw nothing wrong.

Jeremiah was deeply disturbed by this hypocrisy. Judah had not returned to Yahweh "with her whole heart, but in pretense." (3:10) The prophet now saw that the people had in effect simply adopted a more respectable idolatry, placing their trust not in the Lord but in the ritual of the Jerusalem temple.

King Josiah died in 609 B.C. Now all restraint was removed from the nationalistic party which favored centralizing political and religious power in Jerusalem. Paying little attention to adverse economic conditions in Judah, the new king, Jehoiakim, decided to erect a lavish palace for his enjoyment. Built with forced labor, it was to be paneled with cedar and painted with vermilion. Learning of this, Jeremiah could not keep silent. "Do you think you are a king because you compete in cedar?" he asked.

About this time Jeremiah delivered his famous temple address (chapter 7) in which he denounced the hypocrisy he saw in temple worship. To the outraged priests and prophets he cried, "Will you steal, murder, commit adultery, swear falsely, burn incense to Baal, and go after other gods that you have not known, and then come and stand before me in this house, which is called by my name, and say, 'We are delivered!' " (7:9–10)

The religious leaders were furious, especially when he referred to the temple as a "den of robbers." Had it not been for support from some of the princes, Jeremiah might have been martyred for these pithy words of truth.

During the entire eleven years of Jehoiakim's reign, there was no letup in Jeremiah's criticisms. He persistently predicted destruction for a nation and people so given to folly. Barred from speaking publicly in the temple, Jeremiah dictated his oracles to his disciple, Baruch, who proceeded to read them in the courts of the sanctuary. On one occasion friends of Jeremiah arranged to have his scroll read before the king, who was sitting in his winter palace with a brazier burning beside him. As every three or four columns of the scroll were read, so irritated was the king that he would cut these off with a penknife and burn them in the fire, until finally the whole scroll was consumed.

When Jeremiah heard of this, he immediately dictated the words again to Baruch on another scroll and for good measure "there were added thereto many similar words"! The prophet would not allow book-burning to silence him.

After the death of Jehoiakim in 598 B.C., his son Jehoiachin ascended to the throne. Within a fateful three months, following a siege of Jerusalem, he was forced to surrender to the Babylonians. Thus Jehoiachin was taken to Babylon in captivity along with thousands of other members of the aristocracy. The Babylonians appointed his weak-kneed uncle, Zedekiah, as king in his place. With this turn of events, Jeremiah envisioned a new day eventually for the exiles who were suffering under the judgment of God, but he saw little future for the unrepentant people remaining in Judah. Although the prophets who accompanied the exiles to Babylon were encouraging them to look forward to a speedy return, Jeremiah denounced such optimism and suggested that the exiles make plans to remain in Babylon for many years.

Meanwhile, in violation of an oath of allegiance to Babylonia, in 593 B.C. Zedekiah joined in a plot with Edom, Moab, Ammon, Tyre, and Sidon to throw off Judah's new masters. Seeing no hope for his nation in its spiritual condition, Jeremiah counseled surrender when Zedekiah's revolt inspired a Babylonian army to march on Judah. For such traitorous advice, Pashur, an officer of the temple, had Jeremiah beaten and placed in stocks. Even the princes deserted him now. Once he was left to rot in the bottom of a slimy cistern. Through the intercession of the vacillating Zedekiah, Jeremiah was rescued, only to repeat his advice to the king that he should surrender to Babylon to spare his life and save the city.

After a long and bitter siege the city did indeed fall; its walls and temple were destroyed, Zedekiah was captured, and his sons were killed before his very eyes. Then he was blinded and carried off to Babylon in chains together with other members of the aristocracy.

Nebuchadrezzar, king of Babylon, offered Jeremiah the choice of either going to Babylon and receiving favored treatment or remaining behind with the remnant of the people. Jeremiah was not unpatriotic, as his accusers often suggested; he stayed behind and helped the newly appointed governor, Gedaliah, to rebuild the life of the people of Judah. Unfortunately his friend Gedaliah was murdered soon thereafter. Some of the princes involved in the plot fled to avoid punishment by the Babylonians, taking Jeremiah with them to Egypt. There he continued his task of prophesying, sending his oracles to the exiled community.

THE MAJOR TEACHINGS OF JEREMIAH

Jeremiah has been called "the father of true prayer." Until the time of Jeremiah, prayer had been largely petition. But Jeremiah's prayers were often "confessions," intimate conversations with God.

From Jeremiah we learn that *in personal prayer a man can bring before God any deep concern on his heart.* Thus he shared with God his anguish, his reproach, his hostility, his doubts, and his anxieties. Always he believed that God would understand and strengthen and guide him.

Another striking feature of Jeremiah's ministry was *his denunciation of all deceit and hypocrisy.* Jeremiah was particularly disgusted with the false prophets who spoke only what the people wanted to hear. They were fond of publicly proclaiming, "You shall not see the sword, nor shall you have famine, but I will give you assured peace in this place." (14:13) This kind of pronouncement Jeremiah classified as "a lying vision, worthless divination, and the deceit of their own minds." (14:14)

In his temple sermon Jeremiah made it abundantly clear that the temple worship would not succeed in saving the people of Judah. They were doomed if they persisted in following minutely the ritualistic prescriptions of Deuteronomy but neglected the weightier matters of the law—such as executing justice and having compassion upon the alien, the orphan, and the widow.

Jeremiah had yet another message of great importance. *God's law was to be written in people's hearts.* He had been so terribly disappointed in the outcome of the covenant relationship which had centered in the book of Deuteronomy. Although its code of laws had provided the impetus for the reform movement, it had become an object of worship itself, so that the citizens of Judah began to think of themselves as "the people of the book." The prescription "You shall bind them as a sign upon your hand" and "write them on the doorposts of your house" (Deut. 6:8, 9) became formalized by interpreters. Thus the people wore phylacteries on their foreheads and arms and placed mezuzahs on their doorposts. These containers with Scripture verses inside them seemed to falsely assure their users that they would be free of all danger.

The covenant with the nation had not succeeded in redeeming the people. So Jeremiah said the Lord would make a new covenant with the house of Israel. "I will put my law within them, and I will write it upon their hearts; and I will be their God, and they shall be my people. And no longer shall each man teach his neighbor and each his brother, saying, 'Know the Lord,' for they shall all know me, from the least of them to the greatest, says the Lord; for I will forgive their iniquity, and I will remember their sin no more." (31:33–34)

Fortified by this belief, men no longer needed the Ark, the Torah, or the temple to assure them of God's abiding presence; he had written his law in their hearts. With such a covenant men could be holy in Babylon as well as in Judah.

JEREMIAH'S MESSAGE FOR THE MODERN ERA

If Jeremiah were alive today he would stress *our need for greater depth in our prayer life.* The average Christian today prays in church when the pastor leads, occasionally repeats the Lord's Prayer, and joins in spirit when children say "God is gracious, God is good" at the table. Otherwise, largely because of the pressure of time, the lay person does not commune with God.

Though no one lived a more hectic life than Jeremiah, yet he found time to pray. When we hold conversations with God, we need to take a cue from the praying prophet and wait for God to speak to us. When Jeremiah asked God difficult questions, he allowed time for God to answer. Personal prayer is two-way traffic. A part of every devotional period should be set aside for listening.

If we decide to take the time we think we cannot spare, it will mean much to us in terms of less anxiety, greater serenity, and more assurance with respect to our direction in life.

A second valid truth Jeremiah would bring to our generation is *our need for the law to be written in our hearts.* Like the ancient Hebrews we tend to think that the externalization of our religion will save us, that what we need is a new revision of the Scriptures to reform the people, a new book of worship, a new hymnal, or a new national shrine. These instruments, properly used, can help. But our experience could also be the same as that of the people after Josiah's reform—the deification of the trappings of religion to the detriment of the heart of religion.

Jeremiah in his lifetime had witnessed the possibilities to be found in God's making of a covenant that centered in a nation and a church. The results were far from satisfying. Now God would write the law upon their hearts. It was to be a "natural law" woven within the very fabric of human nature, not some external body of rules.

Jeremiah was saying that the individual does not depend for his salvation on being related to some particular nation favored by God. Nor does he depend upon the special grace of being included within the framework of some spiritual community. *He stands alone before God.* Yet he is not helpless, for God has chosen to write his laws upon men's hearts. "They shall all know me . . . for I will forgive their iniquity," says the Lord (31:34) In other words, men will be aware of God working in their hearts as they recognize his merciful forgiveness. It is then this mercy, this grace, which leads a man *naturally* to follow the law from his heart.

When one recognizes this embryonic truth in Jeremiah's teaching more than 2500 years ago, it is a great mystery as to why it is so long in taking hold upon us. For Paul clearly taught: "You are not under law but under grace." (Rom. 6:14) Martin Luther stressed justification by faith through grace. And it was John Wesley's emphasis upon the mercy and undeserved love of God that caused tears of repentance to run down the cheeks of hard-bitten British miners.

At the home of Simon the Pharisee, when a sinful woman anointed his feet with precious ointment, Jesus said: "He who is forgiven little, loves little." (Luke 7:47) He implied that "He who is forgiven much loves much." *Forgiveness creates repentance* and moves the forgiven person to works of love.[1]

A further word of counsel in keeping with Jeremiah's emphasis would be: *Americans need to overcome their false sense of security and seek the kind of peace which will offer more hope for true security.*

Jeremiah was greatly disturbed as he saw his nation following a course of action which would inevitably lead her to utter annihilation. "My anguish, my anguish! I writhe in pain! Oh, the walls of my heart! My heart is beating wildly; I cannot keep silent; for I hear the sound of the trumpet, the alarm of war." (4:19)

But no one seemed to care. The people thought they were safe in their multiple alliances, and Judah continued to follow those policies which would assure her destruction by powerful Babylonia. The situation for the United States is quite different today with respect to her power relationship to the Soviet Union. While tiny Judah, with or without alliances, could not rationally hope for more than a subservient relationship to mighty Babylon, the United States has undoubtedly greater strength than the U.S.S.R. Even so, because of the nuclear dilemma, an atomic war with Russia today would bring the United States to a worse disaster than Jeremiah contemplated for war-bent Judah.

We also tend to be cursed by the same misplaced confidence in our security that centuries ago worked against the best interests of Judah. We rest our safety in fallout shelters and overkill capacity. Admittedly, fallout shelters will not protect our cities, where most of our people live, because the destruction wrought by blast and firestorm nullify any protection such shelters might otherwise provide.

Despite the United States' overkill capacity advantage in relation to the Soviet Union, we are not certain of our ability to adequately defend our own population and territory. "Today the U.S. has about 8,900 strategic nuclear weapons against the Soviet Union's 3,500."[2] Usually it has been considered that 400 well-directed missiles are enough to effectively destroy either country. Therefore, this means that the overkill capacity (the ability to destroy the adversary more than once) of the United States is about twenty-one while that of the U.S.S.R. is approximately eight. With such a preponderance of power there is no way to "defend" ourselves except through an unthinkable first strike. It is questionable as to whether adding to an overkill of twenty-one increases deterrence. Augmented options could simply increase the danger of accidental war. Thus, we are in the irrational position of continuing to stockpile overkill even though it adds nothing to our ability to defend ourselves. We are victims of a misplaced confidence that our arms buildup provides additional security when in reality it does not.

Such a false sense of security can be likened to the attitude that preceded the sinking of the *Titanic*. The ship was believed to be unsinkable. But it went down, and the thing that "couldn't happen" happened.

Today it would be a fatal mistake to be lulled into a false sense of security by a growing stockpile of H-bombs or a profusion of civil defense signs at shelters which may protect against fallout but not against fall-in.

Instead, for true security we should seek safeguarded, world-wide, and complete disarmament. There are those who feel that such an agreement with the Soviet Union is impossible. But, as John J. McCloy, a U.S. negotiator on disarmament, points out, a century and a half ago the relationships of the United States with Canada were just as strained as are those between our country and the U.S.S.R. today.

During the War of 1812 the Canadians had burned Washington, D.C. Forts bristled prominently at the U.S.-Canadian border and occasionally blood was spilled. Despite the mounting tension and over the objections of military leadership of both nations, each side agreed to limit the number of warships on the Great Lakes. Soon after this the forts fell into disuse, and in time relationships so improved that no arms were needed along the border at all.[3] An effective disarmament agreement between Russia and the United States could open up the way for a similar modus vivendi between East and West.

We can be sure that Jeremiah would agree today with this advice from the New Testament:

> ". . . seek peace and pursue it;
> For the eyes of the Lord are upon the righteous,
> and his ears are open to their prayer. . . ."

(1 Peter 3:11–12)

Selections from Jeremiah

THE CALL OF JEREMIAH 1:4–10

Now the word of the LORD came to me saying,
 "Before I formed you in the womb I knew you,
 and before you were born I consecrated you;
 I appointed you a prophet to the nations."
Then I said, "Ah, Lord GOD! Behold, I do not know how to
speak, for I am only a youth." But the LORD said to me,
 "Do not say, 'I am only a youth';
 for to all to whom I send you you shall go,
 and whatever I command you you shall speak.
 Be not afraid of them,
 for I am with you to deliver you,

says the LORD."

Then the LORD put forth his hand and touched my
mouth; and the LORD said to me,
 "Behold, I have put my words in your mouth.
 See, I have set you this day over nations and over kingdoms,
 to pluck up and to break down,
 to destroy and to overthrow,
 to build and to plant."

THE APOSTASY OF ISRAEL 2:1–8, 11–13

The word of the LORD came to me, saying, "Go and
proclaim in the hearing of Jerusalem, Thus says the LORD,
 I remember the devotion of your youth,
 your love as a bride,
 how you followed me in the wilderness,
 in a land not sown.
 Israel was holy to the LORD,
 the first fruits of his harvest.
 All who ate of it became guilty;
 evil came upon them,

says the LORD."

Hear the word of the LORD, O house of Jacob, and all the families
of the house of Israel. Thus says the LORD:
 "What wrong did your fathers find in me

that they went far from me,
and went after worthlessness, and became worthless?
They did not say, 'Where is the LORD
  who brought us up from the land of Egypt,
who led us in the wilderness,
  in a land of deserts and pits,
in a land of drought and deep darkness,
  in a land that none passes through,
  where no man dwells?'
And I brought you into a plentiful land
  to enjoy its fruits and its good things.
But when you came in you defiled my land,
  and made my heritage an abomination.
The priests did not say, 'Where is the LORD?'
  Those who handle the law did not know me;
the rulers transgressed against me;
  the prophets prophesied by Baal,
  and went after things that do not profit. . . .
Has a nation changed its gods,
  even though they are no gods?
But my people have changed their glory
  for that which does not profit.
Be appalled, O heavens, at this,
  be shocked, be utterly desolate,

                                    says the LORD,

for my people have committed two evils:
  they have forsaken me,
the fountain of living waters,
  and hewed out cisterns for themselves,
broken cisterns,
  that can hold no water."

THE POWERLESS GODS 2:26–28

"As a thief is shamed when caught,
  so the house of Israel shall be shamed:
they, their kings, their princes,
  their priests, and their prophets,
who say to a tree, 'You are my father,'
  and to a stone, 'You gave me birth.'
For they have turned their back to me,
  and not their face.
But in the time of their trouble they say,

'Arise and save us!'
But where are your gods
   that you made for yourself?
Let them arise, if they can save you,
   in your time of trouble . . ."

MERCY FOR A FAITHLESS ISRAEL 3:12–13

Return, faithless Israel,

                                 says the LORD.

I will not look on you in anger,
   for I am merciful,

                                 says the LORD;

I will not be angry for ever.
Only acknowledge your guilt,
   that you rebelled against the LORD your God
and scattered your favors among strangers under every green tree,
   and that you have not obeyed my voice,

                                 says the LORD.

FOLLY LEADS TO DISASTER 4:18–22

Your ways and your doings
   have brought this upon you.
This is your doom, and it is bitter;
   it has reached your very heart.
My anguish, my anguish! I writhe in pain!
   Oh, the walls of my heart!
My heart is beating wildly;
   I cannot keep silent;
for I hear the sound of the trumpet,
   the alarm of war.
Disaster follows hard on disaster,
   the whole land is laid waste.
Suddenly my tents are destroyed,
   my curtains in a moment.
How long must I see the standard,
   and hear the sound of the trumpet?
"For my people are foolish,
   they know me not;
they are stupid children,
   they have no understanding.
They are skilled in doing evil,
   but how to do good they know not."

THE NATION ENJOYS FALSE PROPHECY 5:21, 26-31

"Hear this, O foolish and senseless people,
who have eyes, but see not,
who have ears, but hear not. . . .
For wicked men are found among my people;
they lurk like fowlers lying in wait.
They set a trap;
they catch men.
Like a basket full of birds,
their houses are full of treachery;
therefore they have become great and rich,
they have grown fat and sleek.
They know no bounds in deeds of wickedness;
they judge not with justice
the cause of the fatherless, to make it prosper,
and they do not defend the rights of the needy.
Shall I not punish them for these things?

says the LORD,

and shall I not avenge myself
on a nation such as this?"
An appalling and horrible thing
has happened in the land:
the prophets prophesy falsely,
and the priests rule at their direction;
my people love to have it so,
but what will you do when the end comes?

A SINFUL PEOPLE WITHOUT SHAME 6:13-15

"For from the least to the greatest of them,
every one is greedy for unjust gain;
and from prophet to priest,
every one deals falsely.
They have healed the wound of my people lightly,
saying, 'Peace, peace,'
when there is no peace.
Were they ashamed when they committed abomination?
no, they were not at all ashamed;
they did not know how to blush.
Therefore they shall fall among those who fall;
at the time that I punish them, they shall be overthrown,"

says the LORD.

A PEOPLE POSSESSED BY EVIL 13:23–26

Can the Ethiopian change his skin
   or the leopard his spots?
Then also you can do good
   who are accustomed to do evil.
I will scatter you like chaff
   driven by the wind from the desert.
This is your lot,
   the portion I have measured out to you, says the LORD,
Because you have forgotten me
   and trusted in lies.
I myself will lift up your skirts over your face,
   and your shame will be seen.

DECEIT OF THEIR OWN MINDS 14:13–16

Then I said: "Ah, Lord GOD, behold, the prophets say to them, 'You shall not see the sword, nor shall you have famine, but I will give you assured peace in this place.' " And the LORD said to me: "The prophets are prophesying lies in my name; I did not send them, nor did I command them or speak to them. They are prophesying to you a lying vision, worthless divination, and the deceit of their own minds. Therefore thus says the LORD concerning the prophets who prophesy in my name although I did not send them, and who say, 'Sword and famine shall not come on this land': By sword and famine those prophets shall be consumed. And the people to whom they prophesy shall be cast out in the streets of Jerusalem, victims of famine and sword, with none to bury them —them, their wives, their sons, and their daughters. For I will pour out their wickedness upon them."

GOD WEARY OF RELENTING 15:5–7

"Who will have pity on you, O Jerusalem,
   or who will bemoan you?
Who will turn aside
   to ask about your welfare?
You have rejected me, says the LORD,
   you keep going backward;
so I have stretched out my hand against you and destroyed you;—
   I am weary of relenting.
I have winnowed them with a winnowing fork
   in the gates of the land;

I have bereaved them, I have destroyed my people;
    they did not turn from their ways.

LONELINESS OF THE TRUE PROPHET 15:15–18

O LORD, thou knowest;
    remember me and visit me,
    and take vengeance for me on my persecutors.
In thy forbearance take me not away;
    know that for thy sake I bear reproach.
Thy words were found, and I ate them,
    and thy words became to me a joy
    and the delight of my heart;
for I am called by thy name,
    O LORD, God of hosts.
I did not sit in the company of merrymakers,
    nor did I rejoice;
I sat alone, because thy hand was upon me,
    for thou hadst filled me with indignation.
Why is my pain unceasing,
    my wound incurable,
    refusing to be healed?
Wilt thou be to me like a deceitful brook,
    like waters that fail?

THE LORD SEARCHES THE HEART 17:9–11

The heart is deceitful above all things,
    and desperately corrupt;
    who can understand it?
"I the LORD search the mind
    and try the heart,
to give to every man according to his ways,
    according to the fruit of his doings."
Like the partridge that gathers a brood which she did not hatch,
    so is he who gets riches but not by right;
in the midst of his days they will leave him,
    and at his end he will be a fool.

Jeremiah—Spiritual Counselor for an Age of Anxiety

SPEAK FORTH THE TRUTH (1:6, 9, 17)

"Ah, Lord God! I do not know how to speak, for I am only a youth."
Do not despise your youth.
They will not listen to you because of your age,
    but because of what you have to say.
I promise you, I shall *put my words in your mouth.*
Gird up your loins; arise, and say to them everything that I command you.
Do not be dismayed by them, lest I dismay you before them.
Speak forth the truth.
Do not fear criticism should you touch a tender spot.
Fear only the weakness in your knees,
    and the quaver of your voice,
        if tempted to speak in your own name.
Know that I am with you, and that your voice is to be my Voice,
    the words that you utter my Word.

AN ODE TO THE DISAFFILIATE (Jer. 1:7; Is. 20:3; Jer. 5:28; Is. 10:21)

An Oracle Concerning Students and Other Young Adults.

The Lord said to me,
    "Do not say, 'I am only a youth';
    for to all to whom I send you you shall go,
    and whatever I command you you shall speak."

My anguish, my anguish! I writhe in pain!
What can a would-be Christian student do
    in the midst of a bewildering world?
Through the University Reform movement
we urge more representation
    on faculty curriculum committees;
    we want to be in on the decisions affecting our very lives.
Our colleges need not serve as substitute parents.
We are responsible:
    we have no time for love-ins;
    we don't even recognize TV stars!
Lock up your dorms at midnight!
    I'm pounding the city streets on riot prevention call.

Leave your residence doors ajar!
  My love and I are deeply involved—
  in tutoring a ghetto child.
Is that sweet fragrance Mary Jane wandering down the halls?
No, it's my clothes impregnated—
  guilty of association with some hippie guys and dolls.

Just as *Isaiah . . . walked naked and barefoot*
  for three years as a sign
  against the folly of war
so we also provide signs
  through our demonstrations
  against the draft and napalm manufacturing
  before White House and Pentagon.

These, indeed, are the signs of the times.
Can you read them?
  Or are your eyes focused
  on posters with dirty words?
You criticize our generation's civil disobedience
but it was your generation
  which disobeyed the "unjust prohibition laws"
  without bad conscience until the law was changed.
In the churches you taught us several things—
  to love justice and mercy
  to be gentle and decent
  to express international goodwill.
Then, when we reach the magical age of eighteen
we are suddenly told to turn it off.
  No wonder some of us turn on!
Would you really keep the Scriptures
  well locked within their leather binding?
And send us off to Vietnams
  to bomb peasants into refugee camps,
  give captured prisoners the water treatment,
  and escalate the brothel business?
Do you ever REALLY wonder
  why we have lost faith
  in your middle-class values?
  in those who *have grown fat and sleek,*
  who *do not defend the rights of the needy?*

The prophet Isaiah once said
a remnant will return.
We are willing to be that remnant, if necessary,
and start over rebuilding society
after you have destroyed it by your insensitivity.
Some of us smoke pot
to deaden the pain and relax,
But, frankly, we don't have that much time,
the three or four hours to goof off.
As for LSD—not many in the Movement take it.
But we don't despise those who do—
who search for meaning in life not found in gray-flannel-suit struggles;
who seek religious experience not open to them through their elders.
And what's more—we're under thirty!
And while you Clairol your hair
and shorten your skirts
we're going to stay under thirty!
—in our life-style and concepts.
You want us to respect you
but remember, we are the "lied-to generation,"
all the time we're trying to tell you like it is
you tell us:
"The U-2s did not overfly Russia."
"The CIA was not involved in the Bay of Pigs."
"We're not bombing women and children in North Vietnam;
We're bombing steel and concrete."
"The CIA has not subsidized the National Student Association
overseas."
"The Pueblo didn't enter territorial waters."
The credibility gap somehow coincides with the generation gap!

Some of us entered the urban ghetto to help;
we stayed to learn.
You said: "Don't get too involved,
remember who's paying your tuition."
Still, we got involved
and it may have hurt our grades.
The ghetto's so depressing,
it's hard to think in ivory-tower classrooms.
And so we exterminated rats,
secured lids for garbage cans,
tutored Johnnies who couldn't read

—about Jane and Dick in suburbia—
patched up deteriorating houses,
traced down absentee landlords,
filed suits in Landlord and Tenants Court,
organized neighborhood block clubs and
helped the poor to raise their voices.
We went to help our neighbors apply for public assistance
and saw the callous treatment by welfare officials
—and felt the shame.
We fought a losing battle
for the option of ghetto mothers
to care for their own children
instead of being forced to take a job.
And we heard the smug well-to-do
condemn delinquents: "It all goes back to the home!"
They judge not with justice the cause of the fatherless.

Our girls went down to the precinct station
to see what could be done
to improve police-community relations.
And the police said: "Don't call on us when you're raped!"
Nearby a graveyard was moved
to make way for a high-rise apartment
but a few blocks away
the rowhouses of the poor
were bull-dozed to rubble by urban renewal
while former residents fled the neighborhood.
When will you show for the living
the same respect you show for the displaced dead?
Yes, for the ghetto-dweller,
the choices may be easy:
which will it be?
—alcoholic or junkie?
We went into the slums to effect social change
but the only major change effected was in us.
We're different—we can't go back again.
Sometimes when we come home at Thanksgiving
and go to church with our parents
(because we know it will please them)
the ushers seem especially inhospitable
and frown at our beards and long hair.
Though we've taken a bath,

their looks are quite dirty.
They probably think we're hippies,
    refugees from the "feds."
At such times we wonder:
    would they turn away Christ?
    —bearded, flowing hair, dress and all?

THE PROMISED LAND (2:1–11)

The world of the Lord came to me, saying,
"Go and proclaim in the hearing of Washington,
Thus says the Lord,
I remember the devotion of your youth,
    your love as a bride,
how you followed me in the wilderness,
    in a land not sown.
[America] *was holy to the Lord,*
    her pilgrims seeking a land of promise,
    As did the ancient Israelites.
They came seeking the full richness of religious expression,
    more treasured by them than fine gold.
What wrong did your fathers find in me,
    that they went far from me,
    and went after worthlessness,
    and became worthless?
Have I been an indulgent Father, bestowing gifts upon you
    more generously than you could appreciate?
When you came into this land of thick forest and rushing stream,
    fertile valley and verdant hill,
    you were responsive to my grace.
As the generations passed, and wealth piled on wealth,
    did you not begin to think, like a pampered child,
    that the bounty you received was no more than you deserved?
And so, instead of thanking me, you thanked your common sense,
    your economic system, and your Yankee ingenuity.
When you came in you defiled my land.
You stripped my forests and consumed my ore;
    you allowed a foot of topsoil to wash into the sea.
Are you proud to leave your grandchildren such an inheritance—
    deeds to farm land of rock and clay,
    stock in a worn-out mine,
    cash backed by an empty vault at Fort Knox?
Has a nation changed its gods,

even though they are no gods?
But my people have changed their glory
  for that which does not profit."

BROKEN CISTERNS (2:13)

For my people have committed two evils:
  they have forsaken me, the fountain of living waters,
  and hewed out cisterns for themselves,
  broken cisterns, that can hold no water.
1000 pari-mutuel stubs—broken cisterns;
100 stock certificates that have lost their gilt edges—broken cisterns;
100 golf balls lost on the Sabbath—broken cisterns;
a dozen well-worn personal credit cards—broken cisterns;
a 40-year mortgage on a 30-year house—broken cisterns;
9,000,000 prospects for Alcoholics Anonymous—broken cisterns.

THE HARLOT'S BROW (2:22; 3:3)

Though you wash yourself with lye and use much soap,
  the stain of your guilt is still before me.
About the dropping of the Hiroshima bomb,
  your whole society bears a guilt complex.
You are like the pilot who gave weather clearance for the drop,
  and later became mentally ill,
for you suffer from a national neurosis,
  knowing what you would blot out of your mind:
that on the morning of August 7, in the year 1945,
  the order was given to drop the bomb
  in the heart of a defenseless city,
  and it fell on a Buddhist temple in a park;*
that the order read "8:15 A.M."
  Why 8:15 in the morning?
Because that was the optimum time:
  the men would be going to factories,
  the women going to market,
  the children going to school.
Outwardly *you have a harlot's brow,*
  you refuse to be ashamed.
Don your sackcloth and ashes!
Repent, or you will be unhappy

*See detailed map of Hiroshima prepared under direction of the Chief of Engineers by
the Army Map Service, 1945. This map shows completely destroyed and partially destroyed
sections of bombed area. Available in Map Reading Room, Library of Congress.

until judgment satisfies your guilt.
Commit the works of repentance.
    Return the bomb to Pandora's box.

TAILOR-MADE GODS (2:27)

So America will be shamed when its priests and prophets,
    its diplomats and scientists,
say to the atom bomb:
    "You are my father,"
or to a stock certificate,
    "You gave me birth."
But from their foxholes they cry:
    "Arise and save us!"
And from the fallout shelters where they crouch, they plead:
    "Remember, God, this isn't a blast shelter!"
Where are your tailor-made gods then?

VICTIMS OF CLANDESTINE COUNSEL (2:36, 37; 3:12, 13)

You shall be put to shame by others
    as you were at the Bay of Pigs,
for the Lord has rejected those in whom you trust,
    and you will not prosper by them.
Your military leaders have been overmilitant,
    your intelligence unintelligent:
        "An invasion of a few hundred Cubans can serve as a catalytic agent
            for a successful counter-revolution."
        "The Russians are way ahead of us in missile production."
        "The advantages of U–2 overflights far outweigh any risks to
            successful diplomacy."
        "We should not overlook the possibilities of becoming a first-strike
            nation."
        "The Russians have an active Civil Defense program."
When will you act reasonably on facts open to all,
    instead of irrationally on secret dope,
    dope strong enough to dull both conscience and mind.
I will not be angry for ever.
Only acknowledge your guilt,
    that you have sought clandestine counsel afar,
    and overlooked my guidance at hand.

DECEIVERS OF THE PEOPLE (4:9, 10)

In that day courage shall fail both premier and president; the politicians shall be appalled, and the men of the pulpit full of unbelief. Your scientists shall now have their unparallelled opportunity to make something out of nothing, to play Creator. In that day the Lord will say: Where are those now who *utterly deceived this people,* saying radiation is as harmless as living in a brick house—the house that has fallen in on you! Where are those who said "97 per cent can be saved"? Are they among the 3 percent who remain, only to die in three months?

Where are those who relied on "massive retaliation," strike-first strategy, hardened missile sites, impregnable defense, and "counter-force theory"? Do they have any force left with which to counter, any missiles with which to retaliate, any radar with which to review their own ruins?

SKILLED IN DOING EVIL (4:19–22)

My anguish; my anguish! I writhe in pain!
 Oh, the walls of my heart!
My heart is beating wildly;
 I cannot keep silent.
For my people do the stupid thing;
 they are naïve children.
They have no true understanding.
They are skilled in doing evil,
 but how to do good they know not.
Carnivals condition children to look on gambling with favor
 identifying games of chance
 with ferris wheels and taffy apples.
Fathers teach sons how to drink like gentlemen.
Sergeants teach privates how to kill a man 21 ways.
TV teaches youngsters how to use chains to bruise,
 and hands to strangle.
From the school of experience they are taught
 all that the classroom denies.
Yet I would gather you up in my arms like a sleeping child;
 comfort you as a baby with colic,
 sit with you till your fever breaks,
 stand up for you in juvenile court,
 visit you in your death cell,
 mourn alone at your unmarked grave.

FOLLY OF CIVIL DEFENSE (5:21; 4:18)

Thus says the Lord:
"Hear this, O foolish and senseless people,
  who have eyes, but see not,
  who have ears, but hear not.
I see a day of utter devastation
  for those who trusted in their own defense
  and not in the doing of my will.
I made them human;
  they lived as subhuman.
I made them creatures to walk on the face of the earth;
  they preferred to live beneath the earth.
They added their shelters to their homes
  and neglected shelter for my homeless children.
Shelters built for their security
  became for them a crematory.
Their government began modestly with a 100-million-dollar program,
  but the unprotected demanded "protection."
What began as a moderate expenditure escalated to a 200-billion-dollar
    figure.
Everything else had to wait:
  schools not built despite rising enrollments,
  roads crumbling away notwithstanding more traffic.
Then the final battle was joined . . .
  it was over in five minutes.
The innocent perished with the guilty.
Neither democracy nor Communism won . . . only death.
Missiles were launched from circling satellites.
Every corner became a scramble corner
  with no time to sound warning bells.
A few reached their "shelters";
  some not preferring burning to burial were awarded both.
The few survivors stayed in their shelters during the extended crisis
    period.
As a mushroom cloud rose slowly in the sky,
  men lived like cultured mushrooms
  crowded in the dark recesses of the earth.
I saw a man frantically operating an air pump,
  one approved by CD officials;
with every crank of the pump,
  he sucked in radioactive dust.

I saw another opening the flue to the "fresh air" above ground;
the 2000-degree surface temperatures drew into their holocaust
   what little oxygen remained in the shelter.
Such shall be the plight of a generation
   that refined its warning signals,
   but turned off the voice of God.
Despite severe hardships, a small minority did survive.
To what kind of world did they emerge?
   an earth crawling with spiders and bugs unharmed by radiation;
   a sky swarming with flies, feeding on the stinking carcasses of men and
      beasts,
   devoid of birds to devour locusts and winged insects;
   forests denuded by raging firestorms;
   streams polluted with Iodine 131 and all manner of dead things.
Did they rebuild?
O man, have you ever been able to make something out of nothing?
Your ways and your doings have brought this upon you,
   this is your doom, and it is bitter.
For you relied on a Civil Defense neither civilized
   nor capable of defending."

THE HAPPY CLOUDS

I see a world where children are playing in the park,
   where all the clouds in the sky are happy clouds,
where mushrooms are something found in steak sauce,
   and missiles transport life, not death.

PREACHING THE COMFORTABLE GOSPEL (5:31)

The prophets prophesy falsely.
My people love to have it so,
   but what will you do when the end comes?
You make your descent seem so gradual and pleasant,
   like a non-swimmer easing himself into water over his head.
   Pity you, who preach to the rich!
How tempting it is, in your wealthy congregations,
   to preach a sermon intended
   to float merrily along on a sea of mink.
Is the mink so soft as to soften your speech?
Are there no "hard sayings" of Jesus in your pulpit gospel?
Do you speak of sharing Christ's sufferings?
   of making your bodies a living sacrifice?
   of seeking first the Kingdom of God?

of loving one's enemies?
Or have you sold out to the mink?
Do you keep changing the sermon titles on your bulletin boards,
   but still preach on the same comfortable subjects:
   "Possessing Peace of Mind,"
   "Overcoming Your Troubles," or
   "How to Be Successful"?
Gird up your loins! Put on the whole armor of God!
Peruse the Scriptures! Preach on what needs to be heard!
Perspire and inspire!

LUST FOR UNJUST GAIN (6:13, 14)

From the least to the greatest of them,
   every one is greedy for unjust gain.
Bored housewives play the stock market
   as though it were roulette at Las Vegas.
Cotton merchants invest in storage tanks
   nonexistent except for securing mortgages.
Government retirees put in their thirty quarters,
   to hit the Social Security jackpot.
Capitol Hill staff pulls strings for capital gain
Preachers and priests *have healed the wound of my people lightly,*
saying "Have peace, have peace," when raging war threatens.

THE BODY OF CHRIST—A BASKET CASE

Thus says the Lord:
O you Christians, strength of my arm, voice of my mouth, compassion of
      my heart,
step off your merry-go-round!
Break through your monotonous cycle!
   You who raise money to erect buildings,
   so you can expand your program,
and when you expand your program,
   you need more money to erect more buildings.
O when will you start *being* the church;
stop making the church a place to go to,
   and make it something to be;
stop building churches,
   and start being the Kingdom of God in the midst?
Stop making a basket case out of the Body of Christ!
Instead, make his Body active, virile, and whole,
with hands outstretched in service,

feet swift to do my bidding,
  eyes quick to see the world's need,
  ears open to hear your brother's cry for help.

VISION OF THE FLOATING TOWER OF BABEL

I had a vision, a horrible vision,
  of a floating tower of Babel.
But it was not called Babel (though full of foreign tongues);
  it was called Lakonia.
The ship caught fire and sank into the sea—
  British passengers caught in confusion of orders issued by Greek and
      German crew,
  commands shouted in languages not understood—
  a disaster situation, with no communication.
"Too bad," says John Q. Citizen,
  turning to comics and sports page,
without comprehending that he, too, is on a ship,
  and the ship is burning.
No one mans the lifeboats,
  because they cannot converse and transmit meanings.
The blocs do not agree
  on the meaning of "peaceful coexistence,"
while the UN has been unable to define the word "aggression."
For some, "democracy" includes the authoritarian life,
  for others, "free world" embraces oppressive dictators.
In your Security Council
  can shouting between the nations replace sweet reason?
Or in your embattled cities
  can silence between the races resolve conflict?
Your International Court is ineffective
  since the world cannot agree
  on the "principles of international law."
For Asians see this law as weighted toward colonialism,
  and Africans know it as rooted in racialism;
Latins agree its base is economic imperialism,
  Communists charge "capitalism" as its core.
Thus, mankind demands a universal speech,
and the name of that language is not Esperanto
  but Patience and Imagination and Love.

CHRISTIANITY—LEAVEN OR LUMP?

O my people of the law,
would you make your Constitution conform to majority vote
    in every generation?
Or has it an eternal quality capable
    of guiding all generations?
Would you want the Koran read every morning in the public schools,
    or Moslem prayers forced on Protestant pupils?
Then why do you insist on the New Testament being read to Jews,
    or the Lord's Prayer recited by sons of agnostics?
Don't you understand that any prayer acceptable to the vast majority
    would, by its nature, be an affront to God—
        so broad as to be "weak tea" and "thin soup,"
a vain repetition
    like a bored conductor calling indistinguishable stops?
    How can we better train our youth to hate holy things?
Go back to your churches,
    and learn to be the leaven rather than the lump.

POLICIES AND PRACTICES (10:23, 24)

I asked for busing to provide for integration
    but lived cozily in a segregated neighborhood.
I called for the Congress to settle the energy shortage
    and lined up at the gas station twice over the weekend.
I expressed my indignation over the improprieties of Watergate
    and reminded my Senator of my generous gift to his campaign.
I blamed the Arab Nations for raising the cost of oil,
    for selfishly precipitating the energy crisis;
then I consulted with business partners
    about how to raise our products' prices.
I complained about the future shortage of bread
    and stocked my freezer with twenty-five loaves.
I asked the President to cut the military budget
    and invested my surplus funds
    in companies producing weapons.
I called upon the Congress to spend billions on the Clean Air Act
    and continued to smoke two packs per day.
I urged the government to institute genuine tax reform
    and pored over my 1040 to take advantage of every loophole.
I exhorted the church to feed the hungry of the world
    and carried out my garbage twice a day.

I encouraged the State Department to press for disarmament
   and purchased a handgun to protect my home.
I know, O Lord, that the way of man is not in himself . . .
Correct me, O Lord, but . . . not in thy anger,
   lest thou bring me to nothing.

PRISONER OF POMPOSITY (13:15–17)

Hear and give ear; be not proud,
   for the Lord has spoken.
Give glory to the Lord your God
   before he brings darkness.
Must you take every minor Communist achievement
   as a mortal blow?
Do you have to win every hand and every pot
   lest your dignity suffer without recover?
Are there no strategic retreats
   which herald final victory?
No quiet marches
   which raise the last battle's flag?
If you will not listen,
   my soul will weep in secret for your pride;
because pomposity has made you prisoner,
   and placed you in confinement so solitary
   your God is shut out.

GOD LOOKETH UPON THE HEART (13:23)

Can the Ethiopian change his skin
   or the leopard his spots?
How can you suddenly do good
   when your heart is evil?
Can you instantly straighten out when your superior shows his face?
   The pupil folds his hands;
   the clerk shuffles papers;
   the factory worker looks busy;
   the soldier stands erect;
   the parishioner dusts off the Bible.
Do not be deceived;
   God is not mocked.
His presence is constant.
He looks beneath the skin,
   from the spots to the spotless,
   to the center of your heart.

THE FAITHFUL SPIRITUAL LEADER (14:14)

The prophets are prophesying lies in my name; I did not send them, nor did I command them or speak to them. They are prophesying to you a lying vision, worthless divination, and the deceit of their own minds.

O unprofitable prophets! Your feet of clay
   stand exposed beneath your flowing robes.
For you have been saying:
   "What is needed most is peace of mind."
By gnawing ulcers, recurrent anxieties, and nervous breakdowns
   you prescribing prophets shall be incapacitated.
You have been saying, "Pray, have faith in faith,
   and your afflictions will disappear."
By physical infirmities you shall be consumed,
   infirmities not subject to cure by self-hypnosis.
You have been saying,
   "Think of yourself as a wealthy successful man.
   Focus the image in your mind.
   Carry it around with you and you will grow into it."
With a sense of failure unremoved by Pollyanna tricks
   you shall be obsessed.
You have been saying, "Don't be anxious.
   Surely the God who created the world
   would not permit it to be destroyed."
On that day you will have a box seat from which to view
   man's self-inflicted destruction,
   before you are utterly consumed.
Have you not heard of Tom Dooley, who, dying of cancer,
   used his medical instruments
   that he might be an instrument of God?
Do you not know of Albert Schweitzer,
   who, broken with nervous exhaustion,
   in the aftermath of World War I,
   returned to his beloved Lambarene,
   where healing others, he healed himself?
Is the name of Kagawa unfamiliar to you,
   that Japanese Christian, small of stature, big of heart,
   the "failure" who sat out the last war in prison,
   tarred and feathered for apologizing to the Chinese for his nation's
      aggression,
   one with the slum-dwellers of Kobe?
Was his a Golden Boy success story?

So let the frustrated, ailing failures
  be the Kingdom of God at hand!
Not peace of mind,
  but a restless searching for God's will.
Not physical well-being, but spiritual growth.
Not the image of success, but the courage to risk failure.
Not praying for a *deus ex machina,*
  but compelling responsibility within the conscience of man.

BACKWARD PROGRESS (15:5, 6)

Who will have pity on you, O America?
  Who will mourn your passing?
For *you have rejected me, says the Lord;*
  Your progress is all backward.
Thus, *I am weary of relenting.*
You have learned well the principles of mechanics,
  only to slaughter thousands on your highways.
You have stepped up the pace of your existence,
  leaving tranquilizers or mental illness the refuge of millions.
You have engaged your most brilliant scientists
  and applied their talents to works of destruction.
If you will not learn from your folly,
  what more can I do to correct you?
Must utter devastation come upon you,
  that your senses may be restored?

WARS REMEMBERED

I see an America that wants peace,
  but not enough,
because she has known war,
  but not enough,
not having suffered
  the bite of Russian winter,
  the firestorms of Dresden,
  the incessant bombings of London,
  the atomizing of Nagasaki.
When she remembers her most tragic war,
  she glorifies its anniversary
  with mock field battles.

LONELY TRUTH (15:16, 15, 17)

Thy words were found, and I ate them,
  and thy words became to me a joy.
Yet for thy sake I bear reproach,
I did not sit in the company of merrymakers,
  nor did I rejoice;
for truth is a lonely hermit,
  and falsehood has many friends.

HOW THE WICKED PROSPER (12:1–2; 17:10)

Why does the way of the wicked prosper?
  Why do all who are treacherous thrive?
Thou plantest them, and they take root;
  they grow and bring forth fruit;
thou art near in their mouth
  and far from their heart.
"I the Lord search the mind
  and try the heart,
to give to every man according to his ways,
  according to the fruit of his doings.
Do not be deceived by outward appearances.
Do the unscrupulous rich have enough not to worry,
  or enough to cause them to worry?
Do the corrupt politicians or labor leaders
  believe that no one can touch them,
  or do they live in constant fear of assault?
Do the multiple marriages of many movie stars
  bring true happiness,
  or do they so cheapen a holy institution
  that it is converted to a worthless object?
Do the dishonest entrepreneurs
  enjoy the accumulation of their wealth,
  or are they possessed with an unhappy obsession
  that it is not enough?
Now you see through a glass darkly,
  but then face to face.
Now you know in part,
  but then you shall know even as you are also known."

THE ARMS RACE (21:8)

I set before you the way of life and the way of death.
  Therefore choose life.
Would you rather be dead than Red?
Do corpses march to the ballot box demanding their franchise?
  or slaughterers of the innocent stand guiltless before God?
Could you die with a smile upon your face,
  if, by annihilating 175 million non-Communist Russians,
  and countless fellow Americans,
  you could take Soviet leaders with you to the grave?
Would you rather be dead than Red?
  I'd rather be alive and free!
Accuse me, if you will, of appeasement,
  of serving the enemy unwittingly,
but I have your well-being at heart,
  an interest in your future—that there will be one!
The seers of your nation said of old:
  "To arms! To arms for your sure defense!"
  "Give me liberty, or give me death!"
  And they were right.
A former President said to this generation:
  "In an ever-spiraling arms race, a nation's security
  may be shrinking even as its arms increase."
  And he was right.
Your scientists have stated for all to hear:
  unless the arms race is halted,
  1000-megaton bombs will be built,
  which, if exploded 300 miles up,
  could sear all life in six Western states.
Your diplomats have prophesied for all to take cognizance:
  Unless there is a disarmament agreement,
  nuclear arms will be spread among many nations.
Today only five in the H-bomb club.
  Next year, six? In three years, a dozen?
Today Russia, tomorrow Israel,
  the day after that Brazil or West Germany?
Your biologists are saying, if you will give heed:
  a full-scale nuclear attack on our nation
  could render all arable land unusable.
Do you not know the signs of the times—

that at the Nevada atomic testing grounds,
the only plant which flourishes abundantly
is a robust weed called "Russian thistle"!
Is this all you can promise to inheritors of the earth?
What are you doing to the earth that is the Lord's?
To be sure, there are those among you who say:
"But these weapons are not meant for use, only deterrence.
For if we are sufficiently well-armed,
no nation would consider attacking."
They speak with some truth,
for no nation in its right mind would risk retaliation,
the assured consequence of initiating nuclear war.
But what about the nation "not in its right mind"?
How can you be sure that all nuclear powers
will always act rationally?
Can you always depend upon those in the seats of power
to demonstrate restraint?
In your own generation you have seen rise to power
a megalomaniac Hitler in Germany,
a paranoid Stalin in Russia.
And in your own country, a two-month retired Secretary of Defense
jumped to his death from a hospital window.
What about the next generation:
would experience justify more faith in them?
Come out of your trance!
Stop mouthing the same old answers,
though new problems baffle and terrify!

FAITH FOR THE NEW WORLD

Work for the new world, struggling to be born,
offspring of the old which must suffer and die to make way for the new.
Do you know your own offspring?
Will you admit paternity?
Where there was chaos, let there be order!
Where there was anarchy, law!
Where there was tyranny, freedom!
Where there was despair, hope!
Where there was animosity, goodwill!
Where there was tension, peace!
Must the new earth be an idle dream?
Only to those who lack faith.
Every person has faith in something:

in spiritual providence, or a pair of baby shoes dangling in the
     windshield;
in what God can do, or what money can do;
in a good physician, or home remedies;
in a God-revealed religion, or some philosophy.
In what shall we place our faith:
     in a U. N. Peace Force, or national armies?
     in working out our differences with other countries, or "going it
          alone"?
     in the extension of the free world, or military alliances with dictators?
     in granting newly emerging nations the right to be neutral, or writing
          them off as Communist-dominated?
     in trusting the Russians in a disarmament agreement, or trusting the
          Russians to show restraint in an arms race?
     in the Kingdom of God and his righteousness, or the kingdoms of
          people and their wickedness?

THE FALSE PROPHETS (23:13–40)

In the prophets of America I saw a disquieting thing.
     They preached "peace of mind"
     and flurried through another frantic week.
In the prophets of Europe I saw a troubling thing.
     They preached the Christian faith
     and locked themselves in their studies for another half-fortnight.
Woe unto you preachers who "manicure the minor morals"
     while the hand of evil strangles your people
     with prejudice, crime, and war.
Woe unto you preachers who for a sermon begin with a joke,
     expand the Scripture lesson with dull repetition,
     and then, so as to close by noon,
     quickly conclude with an inoffensive generality.
Therefore, I am against the prophets,
     who steal their *words from one another,*
     who are proud of paste-pot sermons,
     who brag that they can preach "Fosdick's sermons better than Harry
          Emerson,"
     who bawl out, "The Bible says . . . ," and proceed to proclaim their own
          ideas,
     who mislead my people through graphic description of "the furniture
          of heaven and the temperature of hell,"
     whose psycho-Scheherazade sermons enable their listeners only to
          hang on the cliff for one more week.

Therefore, I will surely lift you up,
  and cast you away from my presence.
I will bring upon you everlasting reproach
  and perpetual shame.

CONCERNING THE PEACE CORPS

Spin the earth on its axis,
bring forth that day long-awaited,
when your finest young people
    are not conscripted to police the world,
    or to squander their too-much leisure
    on one-armed bandits and two-armed harlots,
    on shacking up and cheap foreign wine.
I see a calendar with every day a red-letter day,
    a day in which to make glad.
Greatest resource of the nation,
    in broken step your youth march forth
    with enthusiasm undampened by elder wet-blankets,
    imagination not yet cast into the organization-man mold,
    energy unsapped by age's toll,
    friendliness unrestrained by practical protocol,
    idealism undaunted despite a thousand "can't be done's."
I see them moving like an army, but not an army,
    these modern pioneers, fully equipped with shovel and book.
They go, not as conscripts, but as volunteers,
    not to wound or imprison,
        but to teach and heal;
    not to lay waste or destroy,
        but to irrigate and make grow;
    not to impress "our way of life,"
        but to help develop "their way of life";
    not to lord it over with power and wealth,
        but to live modestly in the midst, and to share in meekness.
I see youth who were without purpose, now purposeful;
who groaned about their future with foreboding,
    now alive with anticipation;
formerly ingrown and pampered,
    now whose pity has moved 5000 miles from self.

SAINT FRANCIS

After the shooting death of Bobby Kennedy,
  when ardent hopes came crashing down with body,
San Franciscans gathered up their guns and laid them on the steps of City
    Hall,
To be forged into a memorial by a metal-working sculptor.

Today Saint Francis stands, amid the traffic of his city,
  gleaming metal, colorful mosaic,
  blessing bypassers with his outstretched arms,
  he who talked to birds, and served in silent witness to mankind,
  who sought reconciliation with the Moslems
  and peace with all creatures of our God and King.
He who said,
  "Lord, make me an instrument of thy peace.
  Where there is hatred, let me sow love;
  where there is injury, pardon;
  where there is doubt, faith;
  where there is despair, hope;
  where there is darkness, light;
  and where there is sadness, joy."
And so the guns were melted down
  and used to form the figure of a saint.
And thus did they a symbol raise
  for everything America must praise:
The day when builders will outstrip would-be destroyers,
  and lethal weapons turned creative art,
  explosives used to fertilize the soil,
  and pistols shall be melted down to plows.

VII | SECOND ISAIAH

*This indicates new material in this edition.

Second Isaiah—His Times and Ours

Is the book of Isaiah one book or is it two or more books? Is it the work of one prophet or of many prophets? Most biblical scholars agree that chapters 40–66 of the book of Isaiah were written by an author (or authors) different from the eighth-century prophet Isaiah of Jerusalem. Not only do style, content, and theological ideas differ, but it is apparent that the last twenty-seven chapters belong to a much later historical period. Jerusalem had been destroyed. In 587 B.C., as a result of invasions by Nebuchadrezzar of Babylonia, the holy city and its temple were leveled. Some 4600 persons, including many of the most cultured and gifted, were deported to Babylon. There they remained in exile until their release in 539 B.C. after the conquest of Babylon by King Cyrus of Persia.

Cyrus gave the Babylonian god Marduk credit for his victory. He issued a decree soon after his triumph, freeing all captive peoples and permitting them to return to their homelands. Although the Jews had not fared badly in Babylon—enjoying freedom of assembly, opportunities to trade and to farm—still a number of them did return to Judah with the thought of rebuilding Jerusalem and its temple.

The usual date given for the writing of chapters 40–55 is about 540 B.C., a short time before the end of the captivity period. In this section the geographical references appear to be Babylonian while the remaining chapters of the book seem to point to a Jerusalem setting. The vividness of the author's description of the manufacture of Babylonian idols gives evidence of an eyewitness account (44:9–17). His references to Cyrus by name (44:28; 45:1) tend also to define the historical period.

WHO WAS SECOND ISAIAH?

While the author of the last twenty-seven chapters of Isaiah is not identified in the text itself, experts are in accord that chapters 40–55 were written long after the work of Isaiah of Jerusalem. There seems to be a natural division of chapters 40–55 from 56–66. The former is exilic in background and tone whereas the latter appears to be postexilic. Largely for this reason the majority of scholars believe that these two sections were written by separate authors. However, this writer is inclined to agree with a rather respectable minority (including C. C. Torrey, Louis Finkelstein, and James D. Smart) who claim that chapters 40–66 were written by a single author.

We call this nameless prophet Second Isaiah largely because his writings found a place on the unused part of a scroll containing the oracles of Isaiah of Jerusalem. He has submerged his personal identity in his writings to focus full attention on his task of calling the Hebrew people to serve a universal redemptive God of love. The prophet's exultant spirit shines through his poems, which brought hope and courage to the exiles in Babylon. The people were in despair because they felt their God had let them down; they were constantly tempted to shift their allegiance to the "successful gods" of their exilic environment. Into this situation Second Isaiah, the spiritual leader of the exiles, brought a buoyant message which strengthened their faith in the Holy One of Israel and gave them hope that they would soon return to the religious community of their homeland.

THE MAJOR TEACHINGS OF SECOND ISAIAH

There is no question but that Second Isaiah builds much of his message on ideas first presented by the eighth-century prophet of Jerusalem. For instance, he accepts First Isaiah's concept of God as the Holy One of Israel. However, certain other recurring themes demonstrate Second Isaiah's creative and independent thought:

God is Redeemer. In various passages the prophet proclaims "The Holy One of Israel is your Redeemer." (54:5)

God's redemption of his people is to be manifested partly in social terms: the return of the exiles to Palestine, the rebuilding of Jerusalem, the restoration of the holy city, and the conversion of the nations. The Redeemer also works in an inward and spiritual manner. "I am he who blots out your transgressions for my own sake, and I will not remember your sins." (43:25) In fact, he has swept away Israel's transgressions "like a cloud," and her sins "like mist." (44:22)

Thus, the Redeemer who forgave Israel's sin would lead his people out of exile and into the land that was their own, much as he led them through the wilderness years before under the leadership of Moses and his successors.

"Fear not, for I have redeemed you;
   I have called you by name, you are mine.
When you pass through the waters I will be with you;
   and through the rivers, they shall not overwhelm you;
when you walk through fire you shall not be burned,
   and the flame shall not consume you." (43:1–2)

For Second Isaiah, *there was one God and he was universal.* His sovereign power was manifest in Babylon as it was in Judah. "I am God, and there is no other; I am God and there is none like me." (46:9) This was an extremely bold assertion for the leader of a small and insignificant band of exiles to make in the land of Babylon, where the mighty Marduk was worshiped. He proclaimed that Israel might not be the most powerful people, but her God was the most powerful—in fact, he was the only God that existed!

Although King Cyrus of Persia might have thought he moved triumphantly under the banner of Marduk, actually, asserted Second Isaiah, he was being used by the Lord. Concerning Cyrus, the Lord was saying, "I gird you, though you do not know me." (45:5) Second Isaiah's concept, as reflected here, seems to have been somewhat different from First Isaiah's view of Assyria as "the rod of God's anger." The sixth-century prophet emphasizes God's universality in a more positive way—God would not use a foreign power as a direct means of punishing Israel, but rather, by his insistent Spirit, he would urge such a power to be an instrument of justice on behalf of the beloved Hebrew nation.

Yahweh is the only true God; he is unique and incomparable. Second Isaiah contrasts him with the idols of Babylon which, in order to escape destruction during the coming fall of that city, will have to be loaded by hand and carried off on beasts. Such dead gods cannot be compared with the living Lord, who is not carried but himself carries the people of Israel through all their troubles.

Israel was God's own people. The Holy One of Israel has a special relationship with his people. He says to them, "You are mine" and "I have chosen you." He has chosen them because they have been particularly responsive. True, there have been times when he has been tempted to cast them off due to their disloyalty. But in the mainstream of their history they have rejoiced under his yoke. The Lord has not chosen them for special privilege or exemption from judgment. They have a special obligation and responsibility to serve Yahweh's worldwide purposes: "I have given you as a covenant to the people, a light to the nations." (42:6) Israel, then, had a missionary calling to establish justice among all peoples and to carry the message of God's salvation to the ends of the earth. When one considers that during the exile period and immediately following, the Jewish community had tended to turn in upon itself with greater emphasis upon the priestly functions and elaborate prescriptions concerning the Sabbath, then all the more remarkable is this calling to a universal role.

Second Isaiah stresses the role of *the suffering servant.* Some of the most inspiring passages of the Old Testament are found in the "servant songs." (42:1–4; 49:1–6; 50:4–9; 52:13—53:12) There has been much discussion among biblical experts as to the identity of the servant. Some have supposed him to be an individual, perhaps the prophet Jeremiah, or Nehemiah. Others have thought in terms of either the actual or an idealized Israel, or at least a faithful remnant within Israel.

The most logical conclusion appears to be that Second Isaiah is referring to the Hebrew nation. Evidence for this view is found in 49:3 where the Lord says: "You are my servant, Israel, in whom I will be glorified." When one moves beyond the servant poems to other passages of Second Isaiah, he finds many references to the servant as Israel, for instance, 41:8 and 44:1.

The prophet is calling his people not only to a redemptive role within their own community, but, by becoming a servant of humanity, they are to bring salvation to everyone. "It is too light a thing that you should be my servant to raise up the tribes of Jacob . . . I will give you as a light to the nations." (49:6)

How shall Israel "be exalted and lifted up" and "be very high" before the nations? Not by means of violence or oppression, but through undeserved suffering borne for the sake of others. We know that such a people must in the end divide "a portion with the great," that vicarious suffering possesses redemptive power which deserves to triumph.

But the prophet's call, though given nominal respect, fell largely upon unresponsive hearts. Neither the Hebrew nation nor a faithful remnant accepted the responsibility described so graphically by the poet prophet. It was left to Jesus of Nazareth six centuries later so completely to identify himself with the suffering servant role that it is impossible for a Christian to read the passages without his Lord coming to mind. Thus the lofty ideal held up in the servant songs became concrete reality in the person of Jesus Christ, through whose ministry of service and suffering death all humanity truly is redeemed.

SECOND ISAIAH'S MESSAGE FOR THE MODERN ERA

Of such breadth and depth are the teachings of this prophet of the exile that it is difficult to isolate the insights which are most significant for today. However, I would choose three emphases:

God is both one and universal, spanning space and time. "I am God, and there is no other." Although those of us in the Judaeo-Christian tradition accept the concept of God as found in our Holy Scriptures, this does not rule out the possibility that God may have revealed himself in some measure to other peoples. To say that God has revealed his nature in only one way at only one time is, to paraphrase J. B. Phillips' expression, "making our God too small."

The Christian may feel that the revelation of truth in the New Testament is a cascade of living water which floods the recesses of his or her soul. Other religious expressions may be meandering streams or torpid tributaries. Yet all streams do reach the bottom of the mountain, and bring refreshment to those who drink.

"The Lord is the everlasting God," wrote Second Isaiah. Neither space nor time can confine him. Sometimes Christians think of the biblical period as the "Golden Age of Religion" when God was operative in his universe in ways his Spirit cannot be manifested today. However, if God "inhabits eternity" and is the same, yesterday, today, and forever, then nothing which occurred spiritually in the period from the Hebrew times to the early Christian era could not also happen today. Otherwise, God's vitality and power are sapped. God's Spirit works through receptive human beings, and we may be sure that when God seems powerless, he has "looked for an opening" and found none.

"Heaven is my throne and the earth is my footstool; what is the house which you would build for me, and what is the place of my rest?" (66:1) Such a viewpoint cannot permit us to believe in a tight little god who looks down with favor only upon the worshipers in our sanctuary. Nor can we take refuge in a white god who would protect us against conscience-stirring applications for membership by blacks. Surely not if we have learned that God's house "shall be called a house of prayer for all peoples." (56:7)

Nor can we worship a tribal god who judges other nations by their actions but our own nation by our noble intentions which are expressed in such ideas as, "Our advance bases are purely defensive in purpose while theirs are clearly an aggressive threat to our security." Our God is too big for this. Both his judgment and his love go out to all the earth. As Dr. Lowell B. Hazzard has stated: "We can only truly understand what is going on in our times as we seek a God's eye view, a view which transcends nationalism."

A New Age is being heralded. The poet-prophet of the sixth century B.C. sang of the new society his people would build with God's help as they returned to Jerusalem. "For behold, I create new heavens and a new earth." (65:17) God was to play a creative role in the development of the new era.

Changes are occurring today at so fast a pace that the mind can scarcely grasp the facts of change before they give way to further alteration.

Some eighty states with more than two billion people have achieved their independence since the close of World War II. Most of these nations and peoples, located in Africa and Asia, need help in developing political, economic, and social institutions to facilitate free, stable, and productive societies.

The population explosion cannot be ignored. At the time Christ walked the earth there were about one-quarter of a billion people on this planet. This number had doubled by A.D. 1650, finally reaching one billion about the middle of the nineteenth century. The population doubled again by 1940. It stands at some three billion people today and is expected to climb to more than six billion by the end of the present century![1]

The United Nations has undergone revolutionary changes. There are now 147 members in the General Assembly, which began with 51 members in 1945. It is entirely possible that by 1980 175 countries may participate in this Parliament of Man. Not only has the size of the General Assembly increased but also its authority. When the action by the veto-impaired Security Council was blocked, the General Assembly, operating under the "Uniting for Peace" resolution, took on new responsibility and prestige. How the smaller nations, who are now the majority in the UN, behave and demonstrate their maturity will largely determine the future role the UN will assume in keeping the peace.

The Western European nations, through their Common Market and European Free Trade Association, have become the largest group of exporters in the world. This recovery from post-war prostration, with the help of our Marshall Plan but also largely due to their own initiative and ingenuity, is one of the most amazing phenomena of the modern era. Whether the countries of the European Economic Community will now be able to meet the competition of heavy inflow of Japanese goods, only the future will reveal.

Important changes have taken place in Eastern Europe which have significance for the cause of freedom. In Poland, for instance, the press is now relatively free, able to criticize its own government without fear of reprisal. Both Poland and Yugoslavia have free access to Western books, magazines, films, and unjammed Voice of America broadcasts. Under our economic aid program a thousand Yugoslav students have spent a year in this country to gain technical knowledge, and they were incidentally exposed to our free institutions. The position taken by Yugoslavia in the United Nations has more often been an independent one, free of automatic agreement with the Communist bloc. Today, surprisingly enough, Hungarians enjoy more freedom than any other people in Eastern Europe with the possible exception of Poland. Consequently the seventeenth session of the General Assembly accepted the credentials of the present Hungarian government and they were seated in the United Nations.

In the United States a veritable revolution has taken place in race relations. Under the impact of the non-violent direct action movement, public accomodations are now open to all people. With the passage of the Civil Rights Bill of 1964 further progress toward an inclusive society is being and will be made, for we can be sure that the black community is not going to wait forever to enjoy the fruits of liberty which they consider their due as American citizens. As one black leader phrased it in the early '60s: "We have waited for more than three hundred and forty years for our constitutional and God-given rights. The nations of Asia and Africa are moving with jet-like speed toward a goal of political independence, and we still creep at horse and buggy pace toward the gaining of a cup of coffee at a lunch counter."[2]

In the unfolding New Age, spiritual resources and moral guidance will be indispensable. The Christian sees his task much as Second Isaiah saw his: "Prepare the way of the LORD, make straight . . . a highway for our God." (40:3) We must seek to open channels so that God's Spirit can operate effectively in a swiftly changing society.

We are called to fulfill the role of the suffering servant. How is the New Age to be implemented? Not, said the sixth-century prophet, with the instruments of violence and bloodshed, of power and oppression. Rather, he called his people as a corporate community to adopt for themselves the role of suffering and sacrificial service on behalf of others.

Twenty centuries ago Christ assumed this role on behalf of all humanity. Following his example, spiritually motivated individuals and small groups have taken up the task, but the prophet's call still beckons all those who would usher in the New Age.

Is the Christian church responding to the call through its worldwide missionary enterprise? The average Christian who gives only a few dollars a year for the cause of missions can hardly qualify as a "sacrificial servant" of humanity. Yet the church has demonstrated its capacity to serve compassionately in time of great need: assisting refugees in Algeria, Hong Kong, and Taiwan; resettling escapees from Hungary and Cuba.

Another group which has taken on the burdens of the suffering servant has been the black people of the United States, or at least a sizeable minority among these 20 million Americans. They have sought the redemptive way, through nonviolence and suffering love, to win civil rights and human dignity. Like the ancient Hebrews in Babylon, American blacks yearn for freedom. As the Jewish community enjoyed some privileges during their life in exile, so the blacks have been granted some privileges in American society. Now they are asking for and securing their full rights.

Through economic aid to developing nations, the United States has borne some of the sorrows of less privileged peoples. An American society which enjoys a per capita income of $6000 per year feels itself under substantial obligation in a world where the per capita income in many nations is only $100 a year. We are spending more than two billion dollars around the world for such projects as building dams, providing irrigation, drilling wells, sharing agricultural techniques, training teachers, controlling and curing disease, and promoting sanitation. Nevertheless, our total aid program costs the United States less than one-half of the amount which has been suggested as a reasonable goal: one per cent of our Gross National Product.

If our purposes are misunderstood and we are the victims of ingratitude, "despised and rejected," this should be expected by a great power and ought not to discourage us from doing what needs to be done.

Perhaps the most significant government effort through which American citizens are seeking to serve humanity directly and at some personal sacrifice is the Peace Corps program. These 6000 volunteers, mostly young people, have gone out to serve in 65 countries in Africa, Latin America, the Far East, the Near East, and South Asia. They are helping to build roads into inaccessible areas which previously had no markets available for their agricultural produce. They are demonstrating culture of fruit trees, giving penicillin shots, and showing villagers how to build sturdier homes of mud brick.

Poverty, ignorance, and disease, hatred, fear, and prejudice, still weigh heavily upon millions of God's children. Only as the strong voluntarily share the burdens of the weak and the consequences of human insensitivity can the vision of the new heaven and the new earth be fulfilled.

Selections from Second Isaiah

THE ONENESS OF GOD 43:10–12

"You are my witness," says the LORD,
  "and my servant whom I have chosen,
that you may know and believe me
  and understand that I am He.
Before me no god was formed,
  nor shall there be any after me.
I, I am the LORD,
  and besides me there is no savior.
I declared and saved and proclaimed,
  when there was no strange god among you;
  and you are my witnesses," says the LORD.

SUFFERING SERVANT OF THE LORD 53:2–7, 12

He had no form or comeliness that we should look at him,
  and no beauty that we should desire him.
He was despised and rejected by men;
  a man of sorrows, and acquainted with grief;
and as one from whom men hide their faces
  he was despised, and we esteemed him not.
Surely he has borne our griefs
  and carried our sorrows;
yet we esteemed him stricken,
  smitten by God, and afflicted.
But he was wounded for our transgressions,
  he was bruised for our iniquities;
upon him was the chastisement that made us whole;
  and with his stripes we are healed.
All we like sheep have gone astray;
  we have turned every one to his own way;
and the LORD has laid on him
  the iniquity of us all.
He was oppressed, and he was afflicted,
  yet he opened not his mouth;
like a lamb that is led to the slaughter,

and like a sheep that before its shearers is dumb,
　　so he opened not his mouth.
. . . he poured out his soul to death,
　　and was numbered with the transgressors;
yet he bore the sin of many,
　　and made intercession for the transgressors.

RETURN TO THE LORD 55:6–8

Seek the LORD while he may be found,
　　call upon him while he is near;
let the wicked forsake his way,
　　and the unrighteous man his thoughts;
let him return to the LORD, that he may have mercy on him,
　　and to our God, for he will abundantly pardon.
For my thoughts are not your thoughts,
　　neither are your ways my ways, says the LORD.

SIN SEPARATES YOU FROM GOD 59:1–4, 7–8

Behold, the LORD's hand is not shortened, that it cannot save,
　　or his ear dull, that it cannot hear;
but your iniquities have made a separation
　　between you and your God,
and your sins have hid his face from you
　　so that he does not hear.
For your hands are defiled with blood
　　and your fingers with iniquity;
your lips have spoken lies,
　　your tongue mutters wickedness.
No one enters suit justly,
　　no one goes to law honestly;
they rely on empty pleas, they speak lies,
　　they conceive mischief and bring forth iniquity. . . .
Their feet run to evil,
　　and they make haste to shed innocent blood;
their thoughts are thoughts of iniquity,
　　desolation and destruction are in their highways.
The way of peace they know not,
　　and there is no justice in their paths;
they have made their roads crooked,
　　no one who goes in them knows peace.

A LIGHT FOR THE NATIONS 60:1–3

Arise, shine; for your light has come,
  and the glory of the LORD has risen upon you.
For behold, darkness shall cover the earth,
  and thick darkness the peoples;
but the LORD will arise upon you,
  and his glory will be seen upon you.
And nations shall come to your light,
  and kings to the brightness of your rising.

CREATION OF A NEW JERUSALEM 65:17–20, 21–25

For behold, I create new heavens
  and a new earth;
and the former things shall not be remembered
  or come into mind.
But be glad and rejoice for ever
  in that which I create;
for behold, I create Jerusalem a rejoicing,
  and her people a joy.
I will rejoice in Jerusalem,
  and be glad in my people;
no more shall be heard in it the sound of weeping
  and the cry of distress.
No more shall there be in it
  an infant that lives but a few days,
  or an old man who does not fill out his days . . .
They shall build houses and inhabit them;
  they shall plant vineyards and eat their fruit.
They shall not build and another inhabit;
  they shall not plant and another eat;
for like the days of a tree shall the days of my people be,
  and my chosen shall long enjoy the work of their hands.
They shall not labor in vain,
  or bear children for calamity;
for they shall be the offspring of the blessed of the LORD,
  and their children with them.
Before they call I will answer,
  while they are yet speaking I will hear.
The wolf and the lamb shall feed together,
  the lion shall eat straw like the ox;

and dust shall be the serpent's food.
They shall not hurt or destroy
  in all my holy mountain,

says the LORD.

Second Isaiah—A Universal Spirit for an Age of Peace

THE UNIVERSAL GOD* (43:10)

Before me no god was formed,
  nor shall there be any after me.
Is there a God of the Moslem?
Is there a God of the Buddhist?
Is there a God of the Hindu?
Is there a God of the Christian?
  Nay, for I am God, and there is no other.
I am the first and the last
  and all that lies between.
I am the only God you have ever known.
I was the same at the first as I shall be at the last.
  When people pray, it is to me they lift their voices.
Their prayers may be private,
  but I am a public God.
I have never had a chosen people
  except those who chose to serve me.
No person has been elected,
  except as he or she has elected to be used for my purposes.
Prayers have come for rain in drought,
  for victory, and defeat of enemies,
  for length of life, for the mercy of death.
The Judge of the universe hears them all.
I am the Sun God, the Moon God, the God of the Gentle Rain,
  the God of Fertility, and of those in mobility;
I am the God of Moses and Jesus, of Augustine and Luther.
I am the God with whom all people must come to terms, late or soon.
True, some have fashioned me in the image of their ultimates.
They have made wealth their god
  and have been laid purseless in the casket.
They have made power their life principle
  and have lived to a feeble old age.
They have made personality development their idol

*In this paraphrase I do not intend to discount Divine Initiative, but rather I think of it as a given—capable of working through any peoples or person willing to respond. Without response, neither the Hebrews nor Christ could have become *chosen servants.*

and the mortician has hired their pallbearers.
Moslems walk barefoot into my mosques.
Jews elevate the Torah in my temples.
Catholics take Holy Communion in my sanctuaries.
Protestants sing joyful hymns in my churches.
They are all my people
    and those who choose me are my chosen people.

CREATION AND CREATOR (42:5)

Thus says God, the Lord,
    who created the heavens and stretched them out,
    who spread forth the earth and what comes from it,
who gives breath to the people upon it
    and spirit to those who walk in it.
"Who among you will be agnostics
    because they will not try to know the Known,
    because life asks less of the uncommitted?
Who among you will ask:
    'When will the astronauts splash down?'
    'How was the computer programmed?'
But do not ask:
    'Where does an ocean wave begin?'
    'Who programmed the earth?'
    'What happens to personality at death?'
You who are smart enough to use electricity,
    can you explain its source?
Did you really discover electricity,
    or did you find the given?
Have you created electricity,
    or have you merely developed it?
Is it more sensible to believe
    that the earth, the stars, and outer space
    were created by a purposeful God,
Or that uncontrolled forces,
    interacting with one another
    created an orderly, dependable universe?
Can we afford to make science our God,
    a science that would program humanity?
O, you who are scientists!
    Are you co-workers together with God?
Or do you work zealously on the instruments of destruction,
    putting yourselves at odds

with the *Creator* of the Universe?
Are your conclusions not based
  on mathematical formulae and physical laws
  that are utterly dependable?
Are you mindlessly confident that chaos created order
  that order has no purpose
  that no purpose exists in the world
  that the world is fully explainable
  that the explainable bears no mystery
  that no mystery is found in new revelation
  that new revelation will proclaim that God is dead?"

AN ORACLE CONCERNING THE PEOPLE'S REPUBLIC OF CHINA (43:8, 9)

Bring forth the people who are blind, yet have eyes,
  who are deaf, yet have ears!
Let all the nations gather together,
  and let the peoples assemble.
Who among them can declare this,
  and show us the former things?
Let them bring their witnesses to justify them,
  and let them hear and say, It is true.

O China! Most maltreated nation in the world
if you behave today like a delinquent in the international family,
  then the international community deserves it!
For your history reveals a sorry spectacle:
  in the opium wars of the 1840s
  the British defending their right to be your dope-pusher
  and forcing you into narcotic addiction,
  weakening your nation, and destroying your health.
  But at least it numbed the pain
  of your national humiliation
  at being plundered by the West.
The British compelling you to give up Hong Kong
  in a treaty you observe to this very day.
Western wars extracting new concessions against the helpless.
Missionaries being protected
  by quoting the Golden Rule
  in treaties the British imposed
  though you refused to sign.
The Russians forcing you to cede
  lands larger than the state of Texas.

The Japanese, through aggression,
  acquiring Taiwan from China.
Germany, Russia, France, and Britain demanding "territorial rights"
  and becoming a law unto themselves
  while Chinese were treated as enemies in their own country.
The Open Door Policy
  attempting to prevent further raids on Chinese territory
  but also assuring all countries the right to exploit China on equal
    terms.
At the turn of the century
the U.S. Congress passing Oriental Exclusion Acts
  preventing immigration of Chinese into the United States.
Japan in the 30s
  invading and taking Manchuria
  with the League of Nations inert
  and the U.S.A. proclaiming, but not enforcing its Open Door stance.
Taiwan being ceded to China
  under the Cairo Pact of World War II,
  but Peking unable to claim its own
  since, by others' definition, it is not China.
Thus, today, China's xenophobia is well-earned by history
and confirmed by present circumstances—
with the U.S. encircling the mainland with a rim of steel:
  bases in South Korea, and Japan, too,
  also Okinawa, add Taiwan,
  build them at Diego Garcia
      and don't forget Thailand!

While a containment policy obsesses America,
  the Chinese leap their borders
  supporting nationalist revolutionaries
  so inconveniently mobile as to be unbombable!
Today many Americans view China with fear,
  a fear based on war-like statements of Mao Tse Tung.
Is our fear of Chinese aggression
  founded on acts or only on threatening talk?
"She invaded North Korea, Tibet, and India," we say.
But the Chinese moved into North Korea
  only when U.S. troops were within a few miles of her Manchurian
    border
  and at the same time General McArthur was publicly calling for
    permission to strike beyond the Yalu River.

Would the United States, under similar circumstances,
  allow the Chinese to support
  a Mexican raid on Texas without retaliation?
Besides, Chinese troops withdrew from North Korea many years ago
  while U.S. troops linger on in South Korea.
Or take Tibet:
true, Chinese ruthless acts
  in occupying that ancient land
  cannot be justified
but Tibet has historically been considered
  a "Lost Territory" by China
  with no less claim than Jews upon Israel,
  and even the maps of Chiang Kai Shek claim Tibet as rightfully
    "Chinese."
Most striking, perhaps, was Chinese "aggression" in India,
  where after border skirmishes
  the Chinese swept into the plains
  of that neighboring state,
then suddenly halted their drive,
  withdrew, and voluntarily
  surrendered both Indian prisoners and weapons.

So, where is the fearsome aggression
  except in some bellicose boastful statements
  of certain leaders of the Peking regime?
For China is a country
  caught in the nutcracker of a "cultural revolution"
  launched by Red Guards
  whose button was pressed by Mao Tse Tung,
  a man who had trouble finding the "off" button.
Some think that China,
  by supporting guerrilla warfare,
  will tip over each nation of Southeast Asia
  like a stack of dominoes.
But these countries stand
  more like proud chessmen on a board
  whose political, social, and economic strength
  could successfully checkmate
  any aggressive intent by the Peking regime.
Is the American "presence"
  the major factor in preventing
  the dominoes from tipping?

I think not. For look at Indonesia—
although much in danger of going Communist
    with Sukarno in power and
    a heavy American commitment,
it was only after the United States left
    —closing its embassy, withdrawing
    its military assistance, and canceling its aid mission—
    that Indonesia finally went anti-Communist and anti-Chinese!
How, in pride, we like to think
    our efforts are the essential factor
    influencing change in any given nation!

O America!
How long will you continue
    your present myopic policies toward
    the People's Republic of China?
Your longstanding claim in the United Nations
    that China was really represented
    by the two million Chinese
    in the territory of Taiwan.
It was like saying that
    the people of Long Island
    represent the U.S.A.!
And what about your thin shield of atomic ballistic missiles
    aimed at defense against Chinese nuclear attack?
You say that you must
    develop this protection
    until the Chinese become
    more calm and reasonable
    and responsive to nuclear deterrence.
But will a policy designed to protect us,
    while we keep China under the nuclear gun
    make Peking "calm and reasonable"
    or simply frightened and bristling?
Can the U.S. venture a new China policy?
    throw off its well-worn coat
    of a frosty winter's season
    and prepare for thaw and spring?
How looketh spring?
China is China in the United Nations
    and Taiwan is Taiwan.
Ships laden with lumber and golden grain

embark for Shanghai from the Great Northwest
just as they did in the 1930s.
Students from China study in America,
not under any Boxer indemnity
but as a straight exchange
for United States scholars in Peking and Canton.
China grants visas to businessmen and tourists,
and Americans visit China
unhampered by travel bans to forbidden countries.

There are China experts in the United States
whose familiarity goes beyond
Peking newspapers and monitored radio.
Officials of the People's Republic
attend international conferences
on development and disarmament
invited by the United Nations
and welcomed by the United States.
The U.S. removes its menacing steel rim around Mainland China
and that nation's xenophobia
a barrier raised to the West
higher than the Great Wall
crumbles and disappears.

I see a great bonfire on a college campus
Chinese and American students are gathered about the blaze
embraced in its warm arms.
Silently the students from the two countries
alternately throw objects on the fire.
The materials are very combustible, and expendable.
With each burst of flame
a wave of exhilaration excites those assembled.
On the fire goes a giant paper dragon,
and then a paper tiger.
Toss on a Chinese map of "Lost Territories"
Add the SEATO Treaty;
it will not be missed.
Throw in the quote of Mao Tse Tung
that "political power grows out of the barrel of a gun."
Set fire to the plans
for expanding the ABM "thin shield" to armor plate.
Let the greedy flames lick at a photo
of Dulles refusing to shake hands

with the Chinese at Geneva.
Also, let the fire utterly consume
 the statement that China could absorb
 the destruction of a nuclear war and survive.
Burn Lin Piao's frightening speech
 about the encirclement of cities
 by revolutionary rural areas.
Fling it in the fire with one of
 Adlai's addresses on why Peking should be denied
 a seat in the United Nations.
How the fire crackles!—seeming
 to enjoy its feast of inflammatory materials.
Yet the blaze casts an impartial warmth
 on those who gather to celebrate,
 and toss in Chinese firecrackers.
The flickering light falls on fresh faces
 now smiling, now relaxed, now confident,
 now ready to rip out the bitter pages of history
  and burn them, and start anew.

THE SUFFERING SERVANT (52:14—53:12)

His appearance was so marred,
 beyond human semblance.
Is it a man?
 His blood flows red,
 his tears are salty,
 his sweat runs down.
He had no form or comeliness
 that we should look at him.
 His nose was too broad,
 lips too thick,
 hair too curly.
And no beauty that we should desire him.
 Would you want your daughter to marry one?
He was despised and rejected by men.
He knew a door, not as an entranceway,
 but as a barrier to be shut in one's face:
 "Exclusive subdivision";
 "Private swimming club";
 "We reserve the right to choose our guests";
 "Opportunities for ambitious junior executives."
A man of sorrows,

he sang comforting spirituals,
finding his solace in an understanding God
who alone knew the trouble he'd seen.
Acquainted with grief,
he could be shot for a quarter,
and his mourners would see
a white jury grant his murderer a hunting license.
Yet we esteemed him stricken,
smitten by God, and afflicted:
"curse of Noah"—"sons of Ham";
"white and black"—"good and evil";
"pure Aryan stock"—"mongrelized Negroid";
"marked by the Almighty"—"white man's burden."
But he was wounded for our transgressions,
he was bruised for our iniquities.
The white man brought him here,
put him in chains and beat him.
When he was given liberty,
and sought to rise a free man,
he was beaten down again to keep him in his place.
Upon him was the chastisement that made us whole,
and with his stripes we are healed.
As he strode uncowed to freedom,
our sense of human dignity deepened.
As his flesh was torn open,
the bleeding sore of our bitterness healed.
We are healed of our inheritance
of ingrained prejudice.
We are healed of our pride
in an inate superiority.
We are healed of our separateness
that fragments the human species,
knowing now no whiteness of skin is purer
than suffering love.
We have turned every one to his own way.
"It's none of my business."
"Why be subject to economic reprisals?"
"A problem of time and education;
can't do anything about it now."
Like a sheep that before its shearers is dumb,
so he opened not his mouth.
They sat at the lunch counter, quiet and contained,

unresponsive to taunts or jeers of the crowd.
In a reverent silence that spoke of proudest grief,
thousands marched behind the bier of their slain leader.
He poured out his soul to death.
"Scattered shots through curtained windows";
"Homemade bomb ripped bedroom wall";
"Murdered in the driveway";
but they never cut him down.
He *was numbered with the trangressors,*
set upon by dogs trained for catching thieves,
prodded by charged goading sticks designed to herd the cattle,
struck by violent streams of water.
"Can't put out the fire!"
Yet he bore the sin of many,
twenty per cent without Caucasian blood.
"Separate but equal" equals unequal.
"The last to be hired, and the first fired."
"The right to live next door—to somebody else."
They gathered in the house of God
and made intercession for the transgressors,
lifting prayers with hearts and voices,
hearts fervent, voices shrill,
"Ku Klux Klan," "Citizens Council,"
"Do not lay their sins against
who by our struggle are incensed."

WATERGATE (59:14)

Justice is turned back,
and righteousness stands afar off;
for truth has fallen in the public squares,
and uprightness cannot enter.
Woe to those who would absolutize power
for those who deal in code names have much to hide;
who occupy the highest office in the land
but stoop to the lowest deeds,
whose public service is cloaked in secrecy
because if made public,
they would be removed from service.
Woe unto those who willingly commit illegal acts
because they believe proximity to the seats of power exonerates them.
Woe unto those who do not trust the citizens who elected them,
who will not open their actions to public scrutiny,

who list as "friends" those who do their bidding
  and as "enemies" their just critics.
Shame on those who create a climate of suspicion
  and believe the pinnacle of power places them above the law.
Woe unto those who hold the record for wiretaps,
  who endlessly tape others without their knowledge,
for they will ensnare themselves with a skein of scotch plastic
  and be left to twist slowly in the wind,
hung by a piece of tape erased,
  but with their names upon it.
Woe to those who steal elections,
  who for the sake of power
  abandon their ethics
  on the doorstep of the White House.
Shame upon those who turn the Constitution
  into a roll of toilet paper
who use "national security" as their cover
  and agencies of government as their levers of power,
who preside over the Great Assizement,
  separating "enemies" and "friends" as sheep and goats.
Their enemies are driven as bridled goats;
  their friends follow like blind sheep.
Yet there is another Judgment Day
  where *they* sit below the bench
and are judged by a justice
  they deemed too good for their enemies.

COMMON HERITAGE OF MANKIND (60:5)

I have destined the ocean
  as the common heritage of mankind
  so no nation should consider it its special preserve.
You who are powerful nations, anchor your greed;
  turn not to piracy by raiding the riches
  on the ocean's floor.
Let not trillions of dollars of mineral-rich nodules
  blind you to the ultimate value
  of the high seas under law.
Hear this word, USA, USSR and Japan,
  you nations who are rich enough to exploit,
  be smart enough to wait
  til law provides the guidelines.
And do not create the kind of world

where the seas are not free,
where exploitation abounds,
and the powerful carve up spheres of influence,
and the poor take the hindmost.
My migratory fish know no national bounds
and you must begin to learn from them.
For I see a world
    where the powerful nations drill and mine resources of the sea,
    sharing the profits with the landlocked
    and less developed,
where there is free passage
    through all international straits,
where no nation raids the coastal fish of another,
where sea captains know the limits of their catch
    and leave some fish for future generations,
where seven-tenths of the world's surface
    is placed under UN rule
and world law begins to take on shape and form.
Then you shall see and be radiant,
    your heart shall thrill and rejoice;
because the abundance of the sea shall be turned to you,
    the wealth of the nations shall come to you.

THE AGE OF PEACE (55:3–12; 49:17, 6; 55:12; 65:22, 21–25)

Thus says the Lord:
Incline your ear and come to me;
    hear, that your soul may live;
and I will make with you an everlasting covenant,
    my steadfast, sure love for my people.
For as the heavens are higher than the earth,
    so are my ways higher than your ways
    and my thoughts than your thoughts.
For as the rain and the snow come down from heaven,
    and return not thither but water the earth,
making it bring forth and sprout,
    giving seed to the sower and bread to the eater,
so shall my word be that goes forth from my mouth;
    it shall not return to me empty,
but it shall accomplish that which I purpose,
    and prosper in the thing for which I sent it.
For you shall go out in joy,
    and be led forth in peace.

In that day the flowering dogwood shall stretch out its limbs,
    as a many-armed waiter carrying a dozen bouquets as trays;
and the crepe myrtle shall send forth its blooms,
    like circus candy on a stick;
and the weeping willow will arch her branches to the water's edge,
like a woman washing her long green hair in a flowing stream.
And all shall dwell in a land of beauty,
    praising God for his wondrous gifts to the children of men,
For a new age shall dawn,
    and it shall not be called the Space Age,
    or the Jet Age or the Atomic Age,
    but the Age of Peace:
an age when men will beat their tanks into tractors,
    their rockets into mail-service missiles,
    their H-bombs into fusion power plants.
For this will be an age
    when *your builders* will *outstrip your destroyers,*
where resources, once used for arms soon obsolete,
    will pour into schools and cathedrals of healing,
    into teachers' salaries and urgent medical research;
where talents wasted on war strategy
    are redirected to the strategy of peace;
where young Americans are not sent out to police the world with force,
    but to serve the world with talent and friendship,
not to train guerrillas or anti-guerrillas,
    but to train teachers and farmers.
For *I will give you as a light to the nations,*
    that my salvation may reach to the end of the earth.
Let the trumpets proclaim
    that a generation has come of age!
Let the mountains and hills *break forth in singing*
    and all the trees of the field clap their hands!
For the spell of war-obsession has been broken,
    and the paranoid world has regained her senses.
The promise of a new era
    hangs like ripe fruit on a bowed-down tree;
a time when people may travel freely in any portion of the world,
    their humanity their passport;
when broadcasts are unjammed
    and so are roads;
when nations are not inclined to hide their bombs,
    but anxious to share their vaccines;

when scientists may freely trade their information and discoveries,
and no government will circumscribe truth with political theory.
Let that age step forth with eagerness
 as a bridegroom cometh from his chamber;
when every person may speak his mind
 with no knock on the door at midnight;
when religion may be taught to all who desire its benefits;
when no press release suffers prior censorship,
 nor any peaceful assembly is disturbed by police;
when rich nations share compassionately with poor,
 not out of fear, or threat, or contest;
when no land will be a law unto itself,
 but all accept a common rule of justice;
when people are not joined only to their likeness, exclaiming:
 "He's a Mason!" or "He's a Catholic!"
 "He's a black!" or "He's a Caucasian!"
 "He's a Christian!" or "He's a Communist!"
 "He's an American!" or "He's a Russian!"
but rather shall they rejoice
 in the unity that makes them brothers,
 proclaiming: "He's my fellowman!"
 "She's my sisterwoman!"
That winsome new age shall awake
 when all people *enjoy the work of their hands.*
They shall build houses and inhabit them;
 they shall plant vineyards and eat their fruit.
They shall not build and another inhabit;
 they shall not plant and another eat . . .
They shall not labor in vain
 or bear children for calamity . . .
Before they call I will answer,
 while they are yet speaking I will hear.
The wolf and the lamb shall feed together,
 the lion shall eat straw like the ox . . .
They shall not hurt or destroy
 in all my holy mountain,

              says the Lord.

THE EARTH FROM THE MOON

The earth is one.
   The moon knew it before humankind could achieve it.
   Let the moon be our teacher:

You people of the earth are foolish—
You fight over borders
   but where is the border on your globe?
You claim to be of various nations,
   but I see no boundaries marked from my perspective.
You speak many tongues
   but from where I spin you are united in silence.
You are separated into religions
   yet I know of only One Creator,
   one Lord of the Stars.
Look at yourselves as the Prime Mover meant you to be,
   and learn to bless your days
   as I bless your nights.

APPENDIX

AN AFFIRMATION OF SOCIAL FAITH
(*This affirmation may be read collectively, or responsively.*)

Leader:　　We believe in One Universal God—
Response: whose love reaches out to persons in space
　　　　　　　and to families next door,
　　　　　　　to our own citizens and
　　　　　　　to distant, strange peoples.
Unison:　　For no one is strange to Thee; Thou knowest us all.
Leader:　　Our God demands justice,
　　　　　　　fair treatment for the helpless,
　　　　　　　and rights for the powerless.
Response: His Hand is on the scales
　　　　　　　to counterbalance the weight of the wealthy
　　　　　　　and the pressure of the powerful.
　　　　　　　His feet lockstep with those who march for freedom.
　　　　　　　His ears are tuned to cries of desperate need
　　　　　　　and to voices calling for equality.
　　　　　　　The fleecing of the poor, the greed of the rich,
　　　　　　　and the corruption of any in authority
　　　　　　　are not hid from His vision.
Unison:　　So let justice roll down like torrents of water
　　　　　　　and righteousness like a rushing stream.
Leader:　　The Lord of the Universe is a God of Truth
　　　　　　　and His Truth is no embarrassment
　　　　　　　to honest followers.
Response: He is not opposed to science or technology—
　　　　　　　For He is the author of developing knowledge
　　　　　　　and the source of continuing creation.
Unison:　　We would know the truth and be set free.

Leader: Our God has formed an unexpurgated edition of the earth.
            And He says to us: Explore it;
               for it is Good.

Response: Handle my Truth aright, says the Lord,
             For, though twisted, it will never be bent;
               if trampled upon, it will rise clean and lively.
             And when the Truth hurts,
               speak the Truth in love.

Unison: We hear and we would speak, O Lord.

Leader: O God of all Reality,
             Who calls us to the gentleness of doves,
               but also to the wisdom of serpents,

Response: We would face the facts with unscreened vision,
             Choose among alternatives
               when inaction is cowardice,
             Work quietly for the possible good
               amid all clamoring for the impossible perfect.

Unison: We would be wise—as well as gentle.

Leader: O God, whose Being is Eternal
               and whose children live in the instants of time,

Response: Guide us on all relevant issues
             That the moments of truth
               may be informed
               by the precedents of History
               and by the likely results of each act.

Unison: So give us courage that we may decide in the now.

Leader: We affirm our faith in a Father God;

Response: Under whose steadfast love
               none in the world are left orphans,
               and none are born the runt of the litter,
               nor destined to become lost sheep in the Flock of God.

Unison: We will be mother and father to all.

Leader: O, Father God, full of grace,
               a grace that brings persons to repentance
               and sends them out to do good works,
                works performed not for redemption
             For *Thou* art our Redeemer
             Whose grace is not kept in reserve
               waiting for us to be decent
               but freely given.

Response: In Thee we are not the neurotic victims
          of withheld love
          But unshackled from guilt
          We can speak and act with boldness
          in the full freedom of forgiven men and women.

Unison: Our sins are forgiven us;
          our faith does make us whole.

Leader: O Thou whose nature is compassionate love,
          undeserved and unmeasured;

Response: Help us to be ministers of grace to all the world,
          beginning with the household of faith.

Leader: O Thou who dost love the unlovable,
          forgive the unforgivable
          and accept the unacceptable,

Unison: Strengthen us to go and do likewise.

Leader: We affirm our faith that God is Love,

Response: In the One whose love moves inward
          to cast out fear and hatred,
          and whose love moves outward
          to the remote, desolate places of the earth—
          where mankind's misery is unknown or conveniently
              forgotten,
          and to the pungent, cluttered streets of the ghetto
          where pain is too powerless to be heard
          and too close to be seen.

Unison: Keep us, O God, from confining our compassion
          to needs we stumble over.

Leader: For Thou, O Lord, art our Savior

Response: Yet not ours only, but for all the earth's people.

Leader: For Christ was sent into the world
          Not to condemn the world,

Response: But that the world might be saved through him.

Unison: The world is our parish; the world is worth saving.

                                        Amen and amen.

AN AFFIRMATION OF SOCIAL ACTION

This affirmation is based on certain social principles. Let us relate to it not as hearers that forget, but doers that act (James 1:25). The congregation is encouraged to sing responses with the choir.

Leader: In the name of God, the Creator of the heavens
           and the earth,

Response: We commit our lives, our treasure and our energies
           that we may take part in the process of creation
           that we may be the builders that outstrip the destroyers
       Give us not only the courage to be,
           but the power to become Sons and Daughters of the Most
              High.

Leader: O Thou who art the Source,
           the Prime Mover of the Universe

Response: Move us off of dead center
       We who are so balanced
           as to be stationary and inert.

Leader: Almighty God, Sustainer of all Life
       We, too, would sustain the means of existence
       Working for air fit for deep breathing
       for water fresh as heaven's rain
       for soil worth willing to the inheritors of the earth.

Chorus: Let everything that breathes praise the Lord
       Let everything that breathes praise the Lord
       And bring us into a good land
       A land of brooks of water
       of fountains and gushing springs.

Leader: In the name of the One from whom we come,
       and unto whom we return after death.

Response: We dedicate ourselves to a society
           where all children are welcomed at birth
           where all adults are nurtured in life
           and where the aged, at the last, may die in dignity
       We promise to watch over one another in love
           in all our coming, our being, and our departing.

Chorus: Let's all have reason to praise the Lord
       Be glad that we were born
       Young men and maidens fair

Rejoice in the love that surrounds us,
   that abounds in us,
through all life's stages
and even though we're aged.

Leader: In the name of the God
     who made of one blood
All nations and people
     to dwell upon the earth
And in the name of Jesus Christ
     in whom there is neither Jew nor Greek,
     slave nor free, male nor female.

Response: We commit ourselves
     to the political and economic empowerment of all
      minorities
     to providing youth with decision-making authority
     to giving women their rights to equal treatment.

Leader: In the name of Christ who promised all an abundant life

Response: We accept our responsibility to help limit
     the peopling of the earth
   that the planet may not be crowded, like one huge
     elevator at rush hour, that is only headed down,
   We also accept our responsibility for a society, in which
     harmful drugs are carefully regulated,
     and those addicted are helped to start a new life.

Chorus: Our society yearns to be free
     free from prejudice!
     free from subservience!
     free from stifling crowds!
   Our society wants to be "quality"
     where everybody's in
     where none will run away
     or need to deaden pain
     or need to deaden pain.

Leader: The rich and the poor meet together
   The Lord is maker of them all.

Response: We would learn to do good,
   seek justice, correct oppression,
   defend the fatherless, plead for the widow.

Leader: In the name of the one who toiled at a carpenter's bench
     and gave his blessing to the poor

Response: We shall support the right of workers
     to bargain collectively

to seek a fair share of the product of industry
to protect those in dangerous work
to free themselves from boring tasks
We vow to work on behalf of all who have not reaped from the system
children of migrant workers too mobile to go to school
women hunched over obsolete machines in dim-lit factories
hospital workers too dedicated to strike, too low paid to be content.
We shall devote our efforts toward increasing opportunities for creative leisure
that women may have time to mold clay pots
and men to paint butterflies
We support all policies which provide for a decent standard of living for all families—employed or unemployed
Endow us with a grace that feeds more than the deserving poor
Give us a society where children are not punished
because their parents earn no daily bread.

Unison: Give us our daily bread, O Father
But not to us only, but to all humankind.

Leader: Hear this, you who trample upon the needy
and bring the poor of the land to an end
saying, "When will the new moon be over, that we may sell grain?"
that we may make the measure small and the cost great
and deal deceitfully with false balances

Response: We vow to support all actions bringing fair treatment to consumers
How many sticks of spaghetti?
How many sheets on the roll?
How much water in the can of tomatoes?

Leader: The good store tells us all.

Response: As consumers, we promise to refuse to buy
products harmful to humanity
or which desecrate the environment.

Chorus: They shall build houses and inhabit them
They shall make gardens and eat their fruit
They shall manufacture products and consume them
They shall dwell in a land of plenty
and all enjoy the work of their hands.

Leader: Know the truth,

and the truth shall make you free!
Speak the truth
   and the words will set you free
Live the truth
   and a free person you will be.

Response: We would know the truth
   and reject our rationalizations
We would speak the truth
   and spurn the complicity of silence
We would live the truth
   and resist the lure of hypocrisy

Leader: Let every person be subject to the governing authorities
For there is no authority except from God
And those that exist have been instituted by God.

Response: We accept such authority as ordained by the Almighty
when the state helps men and women to be free
when the nation allows citizens to speak the truth.

Leader: We pledge our allegiance to the government

Response: When it engages in good
When it restrains the greedy and the vicious
When it upholds the value of each person
—even the powerless and dispossessed

Leader: But, under God, and out of conscience
We promise not to support the government

Response: In unwarranted invasions of privacy
In implementing unjust statutes
In fighting predatory wars
So help us God.

Chorus: Press every doorbell
Ring every phone
Cast every ballot
Watch every poll
For we're building a nation
That's struggling to be free.

Leader: In the name of God, the Father,
under whom all men are brothers
and all women are sisters
In the name of Jesus Christ
who blessed the peacemakers
And in the name of every unknown soldier, buried in
an unmarked grave, in a place never before heard of

Response: We affirm by thy holiness
                  on stacks of gilt-edged Bibles
                  that we will never cloak the god of war in religious raiment
                  Instead, we shall try to act
                      as though the world were one
                  So the hurt of our far-off brothers and sisters
                      brings the same pain to us
                      as the agony of nearby neighbors
                  We shall be voluntary victims of world-hurt
                  So that, under the laws of God
                      and in the presence of these witnesses
                  We hereby adopt
                      as brothers, every prisoner of war
                      as sisters, every unliberated woman
                      and as our children, every boy or girl left orphan by conflict.

Leader: Here are my brothers, and my sisters,
                      and my mother, and my children
                  Hail America, full of grace,
                      great is your name among nations!
                  But it is not enough for them
                      to fear your power
                      or envy your wealth
                  So let us work for that day:
                  When people turn their swords into plowshares
                      Their spears into pruning hooks
                      and their H-bombs into heat and light for all humanity

Response: When nations shall not direct their warheads
                      toward other nations
                  Neither shall they rattle rockets any more
                  When all persons sit under their own vine
                      and fruit trees
                  And under the roofs of homes they own.

Leader: We will work for a world
                      where nations share their patents and vaccines

Response: And do not spread abroad patent lies
                  Or feel immune to criticism.

Leader: We see a new world emerging.

Response: Where monies spent for bombs
                      to blow people apart
                  Are instead spent for hospitals
                      to make men and women whole
                  Where funds spent for anti-personnel weapons

now go for pro-personnel programs
to help persons enjoy the benefits of useful work
Where taxes used for arms soon obsolete
now build schools, and homes, and subways.

Leader: For in that day
None shall hurt or destroy
in all my holy globe

Response: For the earth shall be
full of the knowledge of the Lord
as the waters cover the sea.

Unison: Glory to God in the highest
And on earth, peace, goodwill among all of thy people.

Chorus: (Sings "He's *Put* the Whole World in Our Hands" to the familiar tune. Suggested verses might go: fresh water, pure air, minority people, crowded earth, drug addict, poor people, migrant worker, U.S. Government, war orphans, nuclear power, Christian churches, United Nations, world peace. As this is sung, minister gives "Clasp of Trust" to ushers who pass it on to the aisles of the congregation. Each person says to the other with the clasp "He's put the whole world in your hands." The congregation will sing, clap, sway, cry "amen," dance in the aisles, or anything else they are comfortable with. It would be appropriate if at the conclusion of the service, the whole congregation left to engage in a significant project.)

NOTES AND ACKNOWLEDGMENTS

Chapter I, Amos

1. Reinhold Niebuhr, "A Critique of Pacifism," *Atlantic Monthly,* Vol. 139 (May 1927), p. 639.
2. *Accident Facts* (Chicago: National Safety Council, 1976), p. 52.
3. Department of Defense, Office of Public Information.
4. Roger Ragan, "Methodists and Residential Segregation of the Negro," *Concern* (July 15, 1963), pp. 4–5.

Chapter II, Hosea

1. Mary Ellen Chase, *The Prophets for the Common Reader* (New York: Norton and Company, 1963), p. 78.
2. John Mauchline, "Introduction and Exegesis of Hosea" in *The Interpreter's Bible,* Vol. VI (New York: Abingdon, 1956), pp. 601–602.
3. *Ibid.,* p. 684.
4. Harold Cooke Phillips, "Exposition of Hosea" in *The Interpreter's Bible,* Vol. VI (New York: Abingdon, 1956), p. 629.
5. Ruth Leger Sivard, *World Military and Social Expenditures 1976* (Leesburg, Va.: WMSE Publications, 1976).
6. *Ibid.,* p. 5.
7. *Ibid.,* pp. 10, 11.

Chapter III, First Isaiah

1. G. G. D. Kilpatrick, "Isaiah" in *The Interpreter's Bible,* Vol. V (New York: Abingdon Press, 1956), p. 333.
2. S. Paul Schilling, *Isaiah Speaks* (New York: Woman's Division of Christian Service, Board of Missions of The Methodist Church, 1958), p. 62.
3. Dr. Earl Ravenal in *The Congressional Record* (Feb. 9, 1977), p. E677.
4. Seymour Melman, ed., *A Strategy for American Security* (New York: Lee Service, Inc., 1963), p. 1.

Chapter IV, Jonah

1. Edna St. Vincent Millay, "Renascence" in *Renascence and Other Poems* (New York: Harper & Brothers, 1940).

Chapter V, Micah

1. Rolland E. Wolfe, "Introduction and Exegesis of Micah" in *The Interpreter's Bible,* Vol. VI (New York: Abingdon Press, 1956), p. 900.

2. Mary Ellen Chase, *The Prophets for the Common Reader* (New York: Norton and Company, 1963), p. 97.
3. Wolfe, *op. cit.*, p. 918.
4. *Ibid.*, p. 942.
5. Harold A. Bosley, "Explication of Micah" in *The Interpreter's Bible*, Vol. VI (New York: Abingdon Press, 1956), p. 901.
6. Charles DeVisscher, *Theory and Reality in Public International Law* (Princeton: Princeton University Press, 1957), p. 127.

Chapter VI, Jeremiah

1. Paul Tillich elaborates helpfully on this idea in his book *The New Being* (New York: Charles Scribner's Sons, 1955), pp. 9ff.
2. Center for Defense Information, *The Defense Monitor* (Dec. 1976), p. 5.
3. John J. McCloy, "Why the World Will Disarm," *This Week Magazine* (Dec. 10, 1961).

Chapter VII, Second Isaiah

1. Haskell Miller and Dale White, *Meeting the Needs of the World's People* (Washington: Board of Christian Social Concerns of The Methodist Church, 1962), p. 4.
2. Martin Luther King, Jr., "Letter from Birmingham City Jail" (Philadelphia: American Friends Service Committee, 1963), p. 5.

SELECTED BIBLIOGRAPHY

Buttrick, George A., ed., *The Interpreter's Bible* (especially Vols. 5 and 6). New York: Abingdon Press, 1956.

Case, Harold C., *The Prophet Jeremiah*. New York: Woman's Division of Christian Service, Board of Missions of The Methodist Church, 1953.

Chase, Mary Ellen, *The Prophets for the Common Reader*. New York: W. W. Norton & Company, Inc. 1963.

Hamilton, Edith, *Spokesmen for God*. New York: W. W. Norton and Company, Inc., 1949.

Heaton, E. W., *The Old Testament Prophets*. Baltimore, Md.: Penguin Books, Inc., 1958.

Heschel, Abraham J., *The Prophets*. New York: Harper and Row, 1962.

Kelly, Balmer H., ed., *The Layman's Bible Commentary*, Vol. 11, *Isaiah*, by G. Ernest Wright; Vol. 12, *Jeremiah, Lamentations*, by Howard T. Kuist; Vol. 14, *Hosea, Joel, Amos, Obadiah, Jonah*, by Jacob M. Myers. Richmond, Va.: John Knox Press, 1964, 1959, 1960.

Leslie, Elmer A., *Isaiah*. New York: Abingdon Press, 1963.

Leslie, Elmer A., *Jeremiah*. New York: Abingdon Press, 1954.

Leslie, Elmer A., *The Prophets Tell Their Own Story*. New York: Abingdon Press, 1939.

Phillips, J. B., *Four Prophets*. New York: The Macmillan Company, 1963.

Schilling, S. Paul, *Isaiah Speaks*. New York: Woman's Division of Christian Service, Board of Missions of The Methodist Church, 1958.

Scott, R. B. Y., *The Relevance of the Prophets*. New York: The Macmillan Company, 1944.

Smart, James D., *Servants of the Word*. Philadelphia: The Westminster Press, 1960.

Smith, J. M. P., *The Prophets and Their Times*, 2nd ed. rev. by William A. Irwin. Chicago: University of Chicago Press, 1941.